MARCO ⊕ POLO

KU-377-630

Travel with
Insider
Tips

COLOGNE

NETHERLANDS
North Rhine-Westphalia *Lower Saxony*
Düsseldorf
Cologne Erfurt
Hesse *Thuringia*
BELGIUM
Wiesbaden Frankfurt/Main
Rhineland-
LUX. *Palatinate* Mainz *Bavaria*
Luxembourg
Saarland *Baden-Württemberg*
Saarbrücken FR

www.marco-polo.com

SYMBOLS

INSIDER TIP Insider Tip

★ Highlight

●●●● Best of ...

☼ Scenic view

☺ Responsible travel: for ecological or fair trade aspects

(*) Telephone numbers that
are not toll-free

**PRICE CATEGORIES
HOTELS**

Expensive over 140 euros

Moderate 100–140 euros

Budget under 100 euros

The prices are for a double
room, for one night, including breakfast

**PRICE CATEGORIES
RESTAURANTS**

Expensive over 20 euros

Moderate 15–20 euros

Budget under 15 euros

Prices based on an average
main course without drinks

On the cover: Where the avant-garde set creative trends p. 50 | To the heavens at high speed p. 43

CONTENTS

Shopping → p. 62

Entertainment → p. 70

Where to stay → p. 78

Street atlas → p. 110

DID YOU KNOW?
Books & films → p. 23
Relax & enjoy → p. 32
Keep fit! → p. 50
Gourmet restaurants → p. 58
Local specialities → p. 60
Spectator sports → p. 75
Luxury hotels → p. 82
Budgeting → p. 99
Currency converter → p. 101
Weather in Cologne → p. 102

MAPS IN THE GUIDEBOOK
(112 A1) Page numbers
and coordinates refer to
the street atlas and the
map of Cologne with sur-
roundings → p. 122/123
(0) Site/address located off
the map. Coordinates are also
given for places that are not
marked on the street atlas.
A public transportation
map can be found inside
the back cover.

INSIDE BACK COVER:
PULL-OUT MAP →

PULL-OUT MAP 〽
(〽 A–B 2–3) Refers to the
removable pull-out map

The best
MARCO POLO
Insider Tips

Our top 15 Insider Tips

INSIDERTIP Retro tables

People of all ages enjoy the 1950s flair of the Weißer Holunder. On Sundays from 6pm: sing along to German oldies and sea shanties (photo right) → p. 76

INSIDERTIP Unlimited fun

Decke Trumm (kettle drums) and *Quetschebüggel* (accordions): the square An der Eiche is the best place to celebrate *Weiberfastnacht* or Fat Thursday → p. 47

INSIDERTIP Authentic *Kölsch*

Once the meeting place for First World War veterans, the Früh em Veedel beer garden and pub is still known as the 'church of the invalids' in the colloquial language. Here they speak and drink *Kölsch* → p. 56

INSIDERTIP Jungle fever

Short-clawed otters, white-handed gibbons and tree kangaroos feel at home in the tropical atmosphere of the rain forest house at the city zoo → p. 53

INSIDERTIP Photo art

He brought American photographic art to Cologne: the Galerienhaus in the Südstadt was built by Thomas Zander and is situated close to Zander's studio and other avant-garde galleries → p. 64

INSIDERTIP Beautiful graves

For more than two hundred years Cologne's prominent citizens have been buried in the Melaten Cemetery – politicians, artists, scientist, entrepreneurs and union leaders. Many of its 19th century tombs and grave stones are under heritage protection → p. 50

INSIDERTIP Little Istanbul

Two junk shops and a violin maker have survived here since the 1960s but the area around the Weidengasse now has a more exotic flavour – Turkish jewellers, butchers, greengrocers and restaurants abound → p. 47

BEST OF ...

FOR FREE

● **Fine classical sounds**
Exam candidates from the music college regularly give free concerts in the relaxed informal atmosphere of the *C. Bechstein Centrum* → p. 73

● **Where it is permanently spring**
The greenhouses with tropical plants and succulents in the *Botanischer Garten* (Botanical Gardens) are open 365 days of the year. Depending on the season, special exhibitions are held with flowering dahlias, camellias or orchids (photo) → p. 50

● **When stones tell the earth's history**
A total of 50,000 fossils and minerals and a thrilling trip through time from the Big Bang to the present: the *Geo-Museum* at the University of Cologne → p. 51

● **Unforgettable sounds in the cathedral**
The choir and organ concerts at the *Dreikönigenschrein* in the cathedral during the summer make for a once-in-a-lifetime experience → p. 37

● **Summer parties**
A 'singing beer garden', theatre acts from all over the world, concerts, artists and puppet shows: the open air *Sommer Köln* is worth a visit and entrance is free → p. 95

● **Open air gallery**
On the lawns in front of the bridge near the Zoo are sculptures by renowned contemporary artists. From the terrace of the cafeteria, you will have a lovely view of the *Skulpturenpark* → p. 52

● **Breathe deeply in the Stadtwald**
The *Wildgehege Stadtwald* is an urban park – the perfect place to get away from the city's hustle and bustle – with deer, beautiful peacocks, a pond and a play ground on the other side of Kitschburger Straße → p. 93

 Dots in guidebook refer to 'Best of ...' tips

● *Underground time machine*

Go underground in Cologne and take a journey into the city's past in the Rathaus (town hall) quarter, follow the trail of its Roman and medieval citizens. The excavations have recently been incorporated into an underground museum → p. 29

● *A funny bird*

Order *ne Halve Hahn* (half a chicken) in a *Brauhaus* but don't be surprised when you are served rye bread and cheese. This authentic dish with the confusing name is served at the *Früh am Dom* → p. 56

● *Puppet plays*

Even if you don't understand a word: the *Puppenspiele der Stadt Köln* – the official name of the Hänneschen Theatre – presents satirical plays in *Kölsch* the local dialect (photo) → p. 77

● *Three days of fun*

'Three days of fun, no regrets, that is carnival' is the local saying about the *Straßenkarneval* – a street carnival and masquerade festival → p. 94

● *Meet the waiters*

The *Köbes* are an institution in Rhine gastronomy and belong to the folklore of Cologne's brewery pubs. To see just how witty and gruff (and rude!) they can be visit the *Brauhaus Päffgen* → p. 56

● *Speaking and drinking Kölsch*

Kölsch is the only language that one can drink. This hoppy, bitter beer is great for a quick drink and is served in small 0.2 L (7 fl oz.) glasses. See how fluent you can be at the *Schreckenskammer* → p. 57

● *Have a laugh in the Volkstheater*

The burlesque farces presented at the *Volkstheater Millowitsch* have kept the locals entertained for over 160 years and are as popular as ever → p. 77

ONLY IN

BEST OF ...

AND IF IT RAINS?
Activities to brighten your day

● **Warm up in the thermal baths**
When the city is drenched by drizzling rain, the best place to retreat to is the sauna – the warmest place is in the *Claudius Therme* → p. 44

● **Body and mind**
Shopping, gastronomy, culture: in the *Neumarkt-Passage* you can browse to your heart's content through jewellery stores and boutiques, discover carpet designs, the Käthe Kollwitz Museum or the Lew Kopelew Forum or eat tapas at Hofers EssBar → p. 68

● **From Picasso to Pop Art**
Works of the masters from the past 100 years in the permanent collection, as well as travelling collections of contemporary art: all the most important artists and influences of modern art history are represented at the *Museum Ludwig* → p. 34

● **For bookworms**
Help yourself to the books at the café-restaurant *Goldmund* and make yourself comfortable at one of their tables. Menu tip: guests come from all over to enjoy their lentil *dhal* (photo) → p. 61

● **Museum trio**
In the *Kulturzentrum Neumarkt* you will definitely not be bored: the *Rautenstrauch-Joest Museum* takes you on a world journey, while the *JuniorMuseum* has childrens' rooms from around the world and then there are the sacred treasures in the *Schnütgen Museum* → p. 40

● **Scientific adventure**
For two to three hours, this interactive research journey takes you through five theme worlds in the *Odysseum*. You will forget about bad weather with their astronaut training → p. 93

RELAX AND CHILL OUT
Take it easy and spoil yourself

● *Relax in some bubbles*
Sparkling mineral water is not just for drinking. The *Ahr Thermen* is a great place to unwind and relax your tired muscles → **p. 53**

● *Cologne's front room*
In the afternoon, when the sun is shining on the café terraces on the *Alter Markt*, lean back in your chair and enjoy the historical backdrop and tasty treats → **p. 28**

● *Boating on the river*
A Rhine boat excursion is a must – boats no longer go to Mülheim but still go to Rodenkirchen – chug along to the sound of gentle waves and soft music at night → **p. 98**

● *Tropical paradise on the banks of the Rhine*
An artificial beach, with sun loungers and a typical beach-bar for drinks: at the *Cologne Beach Club km 689* the banks of the Rhine are turned into the Caribbean → **p. 43**

● *Massaged like a sultan*
First an oriental Rasul bath, then the starlight whirlpool and a Hawaiian lomi-lomi massage: the unusual massage techniques used in the *Spa at the Savoy Hotel* (photo) will certainly help you relax → **p. 81**

● *When the sun sets*
The most beautiful sunsets are seen at the *Deutzer Ufer,* with the shimmering gold reflection of the Rhine. On clear days, the cathedral towers are bathed in a warm glow → **p. 43**

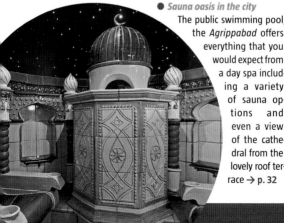

● *Sauna oasis in the city*
The public swimming pool, the *Agrippabad* offers everything that you would expect from a day spa including a variety of sauna options and even a view of the cathedral from the lovely roof terrace → **p. 32**

INTRODUCTION

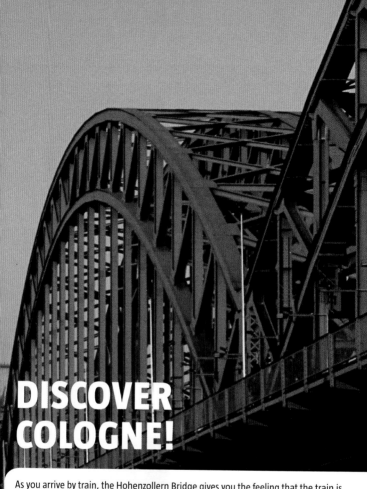

DISCOVER COLOGNE!

As you arrive by train, the Hohenzollern Bridge gives you the feeling that the train is travelling straight to the Dom, Cologne's famous cathedral. Through the compartment window you will see the Rhine with its fleet of white excursion steamboats, the bridges, the narrow houses of the Altstadt and the mighty Romanesque Groß (Great) St Martin church.

Cologne has always wanted to be a major metropolis and with a steady influx of residents, it recently reached the prized 1 million residents mark in 2010. The city's growth can be ascribed to the fact that many information technology companies use Cologne as their headquarters. In 2008 Microsoft moved their North Rhine-Westphalia branch from Neuss to the Rheinau harbour in Cologne – a very important move. The local chamber of commerce counted 11,000 IT companies with approximately 100,000

Photo: View from the banks of the Rhine

employees in 2010 in the Cologne area. This 'network on the Rhine' industry shows great growth and the same applies to their colleagues in the creative industry with their designer offices and media companies in the Ehrenfeld district. WDR and RTL are the biggest broadcasting stations and the biggest employers in the city. Ten television and radio broadcasters are based in Cologne. About 15,000 people work in about 800 media companies.

Media is big business: the creative sector is booming

This is exactly what economists predicted years ago: a positive influence on the demographic development is the settlement of young West Germans under the age of 30, who work on the development of mobile phone applications or as editors at private broadcasters and online services. The employees in these branches have created this economic revival because they enjoy spending their money and going out. They have shaped the party atmosphere of this modern cosmopolitan city with a club culture and bar scene. Most of the bars can compete with the best clubs or bars in Berlin. They are customers who are also eco-conscious and who like to be seen in health clubs, sports shops and health food supermarkets.

The downside of all of this is that Cologne's housing market does not cater for families with children and in the city centre and in its attractive suburbs, the rent is the third highest in Germany after Munich and Düsseldorf. In a reader survey by *Focus*

The good life: the beer garden on the Kennedy embankment

Online about the quality of life in German cities, Cologne ranked somewhere in the middle due to its high rentals and traffic congestion. Using Cologne's motorways is definitely not for the faint hearted!

Despite this, Cologne is still a very attractive and popular city with more than 40 international fairs held annually in Köln-Deutz. With its 16 colleges and five research centres, the metropolis is a centre for education, research and science. This research Mecca is very important to the key technologies of the 21st century: multimedia, communication and software technology, medicine, biotechnology, solar and environmental research. The University of Cologne has 62,000 students, making it the second largest university after Munich.

The carnival has its own economic sector which, amongst others, employs milliners, musicians, tailors and waiters. About 100 carnival associations organise around 500 balls and assemblies between New Year and Ash Wednesday. During the two days between *Weiberfastnacht* (Fat Thursday) and *Rosenmontag* (Rose Monday) you have two options: stay out of the city, or join the party! You just have to know the ins and outs and not fall victim to the

> **Only one thing to do during carnival: join the party!**

typical tourist traps. The constant drone of oompah bands and the mass party atmosphere may not be everyone's cup of tea. The commercial carnival is very removed from the original traditions of Cologne. In the smaller suburbs and communities though, you can still experience a wonderful and unspoiled traditional carnival.

Only a third of the inhabitants were born in Cologne and its Mediterranean live-and-let-live atmosphere has a strong influence on its new residents. In the pubs and beer gardens you will find that Rhinelanders are uncomplicated and friendly and that names and social status do not make an impression in this city where celebrities and the famous are regarded as 'people like you and me'. Even the relationship between the residents and the authorities is somewhat relaxed and informal and generally speaking their preference is for down-to-earth people. And when it comes to being philosophical, they have a saying, *'Et kütt wie et kütt'* which translates to 'what will be, will be'. Calm and composed, they face life's adversities.

That is also how its original inhabitants, the Ubii lived, according to their motto 'Be kind to one another'. The Ubii settled on the left banks of the Rhine within Roman governed territory in 38 BC. As pragmatists they preferred trade with the Romans over warring with them. This approach prevailed through the ages and no matter who ruled the city during the course of the following 2000 years its citizens knew that spiritual authorities protected their interests. All this behind the scenes wheeling, dealing and scheming created what is known as the *Kölsche Klüngel* or Cologne clique. To outsiders this clique appears to be impenetrable. During his time as mayor of Cologne (1917–1933 and 1945), Konrad Adenauer (who later became chancellor of Germany) used the modern form of an expression which translates as 'we know each other, we help each other' a kind of 'you scratch my back, I'll scratch yours'. In their book *Cliquen, Klüngel und Karrieren* (Cliques, Factions and Careers), Ute and Erwin K. Scheuch clearly described this entanglement of politics, power, economy and the way in which sport and carnival associations operate. Today, 20 years after it was published, it is still viewed as one of the greatest works of sociology and nothing about this system of mutual assistance and favours has changed.

In March 2009, the historical archives in Severinstraße collapsed, killing two people. Building irregularities were further highlighted when, barely a year after the collapse, a public prosecutor claimed that the tender protocol for the building of the under-ground railway may have been manipulated, and that stabilising iron parts had not been installed but were instead sold off to scrap yards. This gave rise to an article in the neighbouring Düsseldorf newspaper *Rheinische Post* which report-

Cultural diversity and the Cologne clique

ed that, 'Critics of the Cologne clique now have one more thing to gleefully rub their hands about'. When the European Court of Justice found that EU Procurement laws had been violated with the construction of the new Cologne exhibition halls, the clique of local Cologne councilmen at the town hall felt no sense of wrongdoing because the powers 'in Berlin' had allowed them to waive the tender process.

Cologne's beautiful Romanesque churches are testimony to its past as 'Holy Cologne', but the self-assured, free-thinking citizens also understood that they had to connect their religion with trade interests in order to prosper. In 1288 the Archbishop, who was also the elector, was banned from the city and Cologne became an imperial free city. Later on its citizens seem to have lost their revolutionary spirit as evidenced in a picture hanging in the *Stadtmuseum* which depicts a scene from the revolution of 1848. The local revolutionaries had chosen to set up their barricades next to a wine bar and legend has it that hours later, a Prussian constable entered the bar and announced to the drinkers, 'You can break down the barricades now, the revolution is over!'

It was during this time that the characters Tünnes and Schäl started to appear in the Hänneschen Puppet Theatre shows. They are entrenched in the culture and humour of the city and represent the two sides of the *Kölsch* character. Tünnes is the unsophisticated, rural type whereas Schäl is the refined city citizen. Cologne has always been a city of merchants and craftsmen with lots of narrow streets and winding alleys. Today it is a multi-cultural city with residents who have roots in 184 different nations. This cultural diversity is clearly visible in the gastronomy and the retail trade – in Cologne one can buy African palm oil and Arabian henna powder, Persian saffron and Japanese beer. In Buchheim you will find a Buddhist temple and in Ehrenfeld a very large mosque that is in the final stages of completion. This tolerant co-existence is explained by Cologne's motto, *Jede Jeck es anders* which roughly translates as 'everyone is different and no one is perfect'. Unfortunately there are exceptions. When the German writer Günter Wallraff visited a Kölsch bar disguised as an African, he had a very hostile reception.

Cologne is an ancient city with a history that goes back almost 2000 years when the settlement on the left Rhine bank became the foundation for first a Roman and then a medieval city. Cologne's excavations have recently been declared an Archaeological Zone and include, among others, the remains of a medieval Jewish ritual bath underneath the town hall and the remains of a Roman sewer system. The right Rhine

The right bank cityscape with Köln Triangle and the Deutzer Bahnhof

bank has always been seen as the *Schäl Sick* (cross-eyed side) because the horses that used to pull the cargo barges upstream along the river, had to wear blinkers which eventually made them go cross-eyed. According to the Romans, the Barbarians lived on the 'cross-eyed' side, and even as recently as the last century those from the right bank of the Rhine were judged in an unflattering light. 'Bolshevism start-

The right side no longer the wrong side

ed in Köln-Deutz,' said mayor Konrad Adenauer. However, in recent times, the right bank Rhine suburbs of Deutz and Kalk are viewed in a more positive light. This is mainly due to new developments like the multi-purpose Lanxess Arena, the town hall, the new police headquarters and the train station Köln-Deutz. Now the only reminder of earlier times is the name of the bar in the Hyatt Regency: the *Schäl-Sick*. By the way, a coffee on the terrace of the hotel gives you a picture-perfect view of the Rhine. The impressive skyline with the cathedral, the Museum Ludwig, the Rheingarten and the historic town houses are typical of Cologne.

WHAT'S HOT

1 Cutting edge culinary

Exotic is hot Cologne's gastronomes have discovered the exotic. At the *Goldschläger (Hans-Böckler-Platz 1–3)* you will find Caipirinha Salmon on the menu and at *Madame Miammiam (Antwerpener Straße 39, photo)* your sugary treat can be an edible pin-up girl. At *Osman 30* the chef serves up sea bass teamed with a pea flan, while the guests enjoy the view from the Cologne Tower *(Mediapark 8)*.

2 Playground

Sporting spirit is everywhere and the whole city is a golf course – be it on top of skyscraper roofs, open fields or even on the banks of the river – the Cross Golf Community (urban golfers) is there *(www.crossgolf.com)*. Nothing stops the traceurs as walls, stairs and bridges become an urban parkour course *(www.parkourone.de)* and you can watch youths playing streetball (a form of basketball) in the streets at the *Nike Court (Hansemannstraße, Ehrenfeld)* and at the *GEW Energy Dome (Widdersdorfer Straße)*.

3 City of art

Cologne art A group called *Colorrevolution* wanted to give some life to Cologne's facades so they collaborated with the city to invite international artists to place their works in public spaces *(www.goodlack-art.de, photo)*. Even though it is not in a public space, a visit to the *Galerie 30works* provides one with an overview of the newest in street art *(Antwerpener Straße 42, www.30works.de)*. The art collaboration *Lichtfaktor* creates pictures and videos from light *(www.lichtfaktor.eu)*. Angie Hiesl in collaboration with Roland Kaiser developed the interdisciplinary urban art project *Urban-City-Urban (www.angiehiesl.de)*.

Shop till you drop

Boutique fans The Belgian Quarter is not only known for its galleries and clubs, but also for its trendy fashion boutiques. At *Erdbeeren im Winter* young local and international designers sell their clothes *(Antwerpener Straße 18, www.erdbeeren-im-winter.de)*. In their shop *Blauer Montag* Nina Hempel and Moni Wallberg sell their own designs as well as those of other young up-and-coming designers *(Limburger Straße 6, www.blauer-montag.com)*. If you want to keep your shopping loot clean then visit *RockOn.de Cleanicum*, a fun combination between a laundromat and a street boutique *(Brüsseler Straße 74–76, www.rockon.de)*. The organisation *Le Bloc Mode und Design* in the Belgian Quarter has live performances and fashion shows with a lot of flair *(www.lebloc.de, photo)*.

Nightlife

Great option A bar, a café, a hostel and a theatre: the conveniently located *Wohngemeinschaft* has a lot to offer with four very different rooms with flowery carpets, DJs and even ping-pong tables *(Richard-Wagner-Straße 39, www.die-wohngemeinschaft.net)*. *Edelpink* is a colourful and loud disco and bar. Visitors must be prepared for a few surprises *(Brabanter Straße 9)*! The purist *Ucon Lodge* on the other hand, seems to be from another world. Water in all its different states is the theme of this cool spot *(Von-Werth-Straße 48–50, www.ucon-lodge.de, photo)*.

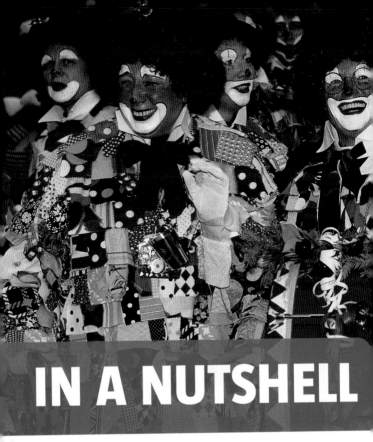

IN A NUTSHELL

A LTERNATIVE CARNIVAL
During the Middle Ages the carnival was used as a vehicle to symbolically turn the rigid feudal system on its head and its participants took as many liberties as possible, then in the 19th century the city militia used it as an opportunity to make fun of the occupying Prussians and their militarism. This anarchistic and subversive character of the carnival has now almost completely disappeared.

However, in 1930 the city's artists celebrated carnival with their own hobo or scoundrel fancy-dress ball. Instead of smart tailcoats and ball gowns the participants dress up in rags. This artists'

carnival, the *Ahl Säu* or old sow parade follows behind the official Rose Monday parade. Another 'alternative' carnival specialises in wicked satirical attacks on the local authorities is the *Stunksitzung* (literal translation is 'stink meeting') which was created by students 1984. It takes the form of cabaret-style performances and its biting sarcasm and sharp wit has inspired many younger people to take part in the carnival. All 40 *Stunksitzung* performances are sold out weeks in advance. The Ghost Parade is another 'alternative' parade; it starts with the onset of darkness on Carnival Saturday and has the *Ähzebär*, a straw figure that personi-

Why the *Ähzebär* is set alight, why the locals love their *veedel* (traditional neighbourhoods) so much and the origins of the Cologne clique

fies winter. At midnight, the *Ähzebär* is set alight.

CLIQUE

What in Cologne is called a clique is known as 'networking' in the rest of the world. This historically entrenched form of cronyism is an opaque and complex network of personal relations with mutual benefits. You scratch my back and I'll scratch yours. This tendency towards behind the scenes wheeling and dealing developed very strongly in Cologne where for centuries the city tried to resist all unwanted influences from penetrating their city walls. An example would be the medieval painters' guild: they divided their commissioned work exclusively amongst fellow members – craftsmen from outside had no chance of being included. Thus the rules of the 'game' were established over the centuries. One of these unwritten rules is that certain matters are not settled in public but in private and this is when personal contacts rative events – that says that the best that a man has is his *Veedel* or his neighbourhood. This song epitomises the special emotional sensitivity of the Cologne spirit of belonging. People identify strongly with

An address becomes a trademark: Glockengasse 4711

come in handy, in the carnival or any other club or association.

This is quite harmless in ordinary everyday situations, but in political situations it can quickly lead to corruption. This system of backhanders seems very entrenched: once when a mayor had to resign because he had taken out a loan from a bank – without any apparent means of paying it back – the local opinion was that he was 'one of ours' and could therefore do no wrong.

COLOGNE'S VEEDEL

There is a song by the local band Bläck Fööss – often sung at official commemo-

their neighbourhoods and this sense of belonging offers a calming influence and haven from an otherwise incomprehensible and stormy world. This patriotic sentiment applies across the social scale from expensive residential areas like Marienburg, or a peaceful suburb like Dellbrück or the multi-cultural Eigelstein Quarter.

COMEDY

The *Stunksitzung* has developed into a springboard for many cabaret and comedy careers. The ex-member Jürgen Becker is now a presenter for *Mitternachtsspitzen* a comedy show on WDR Television. Wilfried Schmickler, who performed with Becker in the alternative troupe *3Gestirn* received the German cabaret award in 2009. This new generation of comedians still take part in both the festival Köln Comedy Cup (July) and the Köln Festival (October) but very few have made the jump to television. With comedy steadily waning, cabaret artists are more in the spotlight: from the neighbouring city of Bonn, Norbert Alich and Rainer Pause regularly travel to perform in Cologne's *Senftöpfchen* and they also have their own show *Fritz und Herman* on WDR. Pause also performs with Martin Stankowski in Cologne's funeral homes where they illustrate the local funeral rituals in a humorous way with *Tod im Rheinland*.

E AU DE COLOGNE

In 1794 a general in the occupying French army had all the buildings in Cologne numbered. Wilhelm Mühlens home in the Glockengasse alley was given the number 4711. A house number which is still in use to this day. Pop in and refresh yourself at the 4711 fountain by the doorway. The production of this distillation of alcohol and blossom oil started in 1709. The secret recipe was passed on to Wilhelm Mühlens in 1792 as a wedding gift and was originally marketed as miracle water for headaches, heart palpitations and even to ward off the plague. When, in 1810, Napoleon demanded the disclosure of all medicinal formulas, Mühlens kept his secret by marketing his fragrant water as a perfume with refreshing qualities.

E CONOMY

Cologne's economic potential lies in its importance as an automotive city: in 1929 the mayor Konrad Adenauer convinced Henry Ford, to move the production line of his vehicles for the German market from Berlin to the Rhine. Adenauer offered Ford a 42 acres piece of land in the suburb Niehl where Ford Fiestas are still built today. With its 17,000 employees, the Ford factory is the city's largest employer, after the city council. Toyota Germany has been based in Köln-Marsdorf since 1971, where 1000 employees handle the distribution.

The headquarters of the engine manufacturers Deutz AG is in Köln-Porz where both research and the development of compact engines take place. The logistical centre of the company is based in Kalk which stocks 80,000 component parts and in the Deutz district, where engines have been manufactured (and still are) since 1869, when Nikolaus Otto, the inventor of the internal combustion engine and his partner Eugen Langen started the first engine factory in the world. Before starting his own business Gottlieb Daimler worked here as a technical director. The entrepreneurial spirit in the engineering field helped the city to prosper economically during the golden age of industry. From 1893 Deutz also started building locomotives and the world's first ever fire engine with a combustion engine left the factory in 1903. During the 1920s they also began to mass produce tractors.

Automotive and engine production still plays an important role in Cologne's economy, even though the potential for future development lies mainly in the services and media industries. But, as in the past, certain traditional businesses still provide services to many people in the city. Pfeifer & Langen the producers of the famous Cologne sugar and the third largest German sugar producer, have 850 employees in Cologne. In 1851, one of the company's founders Emil Pfeifer was the first to discover that sugar could be produced from beets.

HUMOUR

'Fear evoking' is how Nobel literature laureate Heinrich Böll described the Cologne sense of humour in its official form. He was referring to the smug and somewhat conceited behaviour of the carnival jesters and the banter indulged in by the city's people in high places. However, it was on the streets that Böll experienced the true Cologne humour as erence for crudeness. Ones sense of humour, by contrast, is embedded in ones psyche and has absolutely nothing to do with corny professional comics. Böll's Everyman is no stranger to his own weaknesses and shortcomings.

A popular Cologne local Cardinal Josef Frings once pointed out: that nothing human was strange to him. In the words of Heinrich Lützeler: 'Those in need of

Cologne's famous figures Tünnes and Schäl

an expression 'of greatness and wisdom'. Bonn art historian Heinrich Lützeler even wrote a book entitled *Philosophy of Cologne Humour* in which he makes a distinction between jokes and a sense of humour.

If you follow the reasoning of this distinction you will have an understanding of what Böll meant: a joke is an intellectual construction, usually lacking in subtlety in Cologne's society where there is a pref-empathy will have empathy for others. Whoever is not intrinsically good is more kind-hearted when judging others. The legendary characters Tünnes and Schäl are not exemplary. They do not conform to the book of ideals but to the book of life'.

KÖLSCHROCK

At the end of the 1960s, the Stowaways were one of the many bands from Cologne who sang in English, they changed their name to Bläck Fööss (bare feet) in 1970 and started to singing in Kölsch, the local dialect. They revolutionised the carnival with their music, which up until then only had a repertoire of waltzes and marching bands. After leaving the band, Tommy Engel together with Arno Steffen and Rolf Lammers started the trio L.S.E. in 1992.

Gerd Köster is regarded as Cologne's Tom Waits. The band Brings had a best seller in 2001 with their hit *Supergeile Zick* (a great time) but it was Wolfgang Niedecken and his band BAP that made *Kölschrock* famous throughout Germany. In the early 1980s their songs like *Verdamp lang her* (damn long time) with its uncomplicated rock sound paved the way on German radio stations. The word BAP is a play on the local variant for the word 'daddy'. Only Wolfgang Niedecken is left from the original band lineup and his lyrics critiquing politics are still very relevant.

MEDIA CITY

Cologne's art and media college (Kunsthochschule für Medien) is unique in Germany and almost a third of all the public broadcaster's television programmes come from Cologne's WDR studios: like the *Tatort* series from Cologne or the *Lindenstraße* soap, which takes place in Munich. Many television crime scenes are filmed on the streets of Cologne.

Not only does RTL produce soaps and series but also Vox, Super RTL and the news channel Phoenix. On average, two TV teams are constantly filming in Cologne's streets – to the chagrin of the inhabitants who have to give up their parking spaces.

BOOKS & FILMS

▶ **The Lost Honour of Katharina Blum** – is a novel by Nobel laureate Heinrich Böll that has Cologne as its backdrop. The story is set in the 1970s at the height of the panic around the terrorist group the Red Army Faction. The novel was also made into a movie in 1984 which starred Kris Kristofferson

▶ **Death and the Devil** – is a novel by Frank Schätzing who achieved international fame with his ecological thriller *The Swarm*. A mystery, *Death and the Devil* was his debut novel. It is set in 13th century Cologne and is a fascinating portrayal of medieval life and the political events of the time with a plot against the Archbishop of Cologne

▶ **Edelweiss Pirates** – Niko von Glasow's 2005 emotional and enigmatic film centres around a youth resistance group during the Second World War. The action takes place in and around Cologne. German with English subtitles

▶ **Ode to Cologne** – is a Wim Wenders documentary about the Cologne based band BAP. Using archive material and news clips the film traces the rock band's evolution and social commentary (2001)

▶ **Fools** – Director Tom Schreiber used the Cologne carnival as backdrop for this absurd mixture of comedy and crime (2003)

THE PERFECT DAY
Cologne in 24 hours

08:00am **ALL ROADS START AT THE DOM**

The main attraction and centre of the city is the world famous cathedral or *Dom* → p. 30. Here and at *Roncalliplatz* → p. 32 is where the heart of the city beats the strongest and is where you should start your exploration of the city. But not before you have started the day with breakfast and a view of the cathedral at *Café Reichard* → p. 57 then climb the belltower for a wonderful view of Cologne from above.

10:00am **THE BRIDGES ALONG THE RIVER**

From the heart of the city to its main artery: since the completion of the Rhine tunnel in the 1980s, this metropolis can really call itself 'Cologne on the Rhine'. From Heinrich-Böll Platz at the Museum Ludwig take the steps down to the banks of the river. Take a stroll through the *Rheingarten* → p. 33 underneath the Deutzer Bridge to the historical swing bridge in front of the *Schokoladenmuseum* → p. 48. Now you need to decide whether to discover Cologne's sweet side at the Chocolate Museum or take a sightseeing cruise on the Rhine (photo left) as you walk past their mooring place.

11:30am **TRAVEL TROUGH TIME**

Take a trip back in time. In the Rheingasse, not far from the Chocolate Museum, you will find one of the oldest houses in Cologne, the pretty *Overstolzenhaus* → p. 35. Only a stone's throw away is *St Maria im Kapitol* → p. 37 and the Dreikönigenpforte gate is at the south end of the square. It is known as the 'Gate of the Three Wise Men' because legend has it that the remains of these holy men were brought to Cologne in 1164. However, the gate was only built in 1296.

00:15pm **BALLROOM, BEER GARDEN AND A TOWN HALL**

Before visiting the *Ballhaus Gürzenich* → p. 33 (photo right) where the announcement of the carnival's triumvirate is the highlight of the festivities, have lunch in the brewery pub *Malzmühle* → p. 56 and experience Cologne's lifestyle first-hand. Later take a stroll past Gürzenich and the ruin of St Alban, which, after being destroyed during the Second World War, was left in its current

Get to know the best of Cologne – right in the city centre, in a relaxed way and all in a single day

state to serve as a memorial. Then pass the *Rathaus* → p. 35 or town hall with its large 'Piazetta' hall and its *Cloud* artwork by Hann Triet.

01:45pm MASTER WORKS

Just how far back Cologne's history stretches can be experienced during one of the exciting underground tours through the *Archaeological Zone* → p. 29, which includes the Roman *Praetorium* → p. 35 and the Jewish ritual baths, the *Mikveh* → p. 33. In the *Wallraf-Richartz-Museum & Fondation Corboud* → p. 37 admire some of the greatest artworks in art history from Rembrandt to Renoir.

03:15pm SHOPPING

Back to the present: the *Neumarkt* → p. 62 and *Neumarkt-Galerie* → p. 68 is one of Cologne's most vibrant places. Here in the heart of the shopping zone, you can shop or browse till you drop. Do not be startled at the two horses' heads looking at you from the façade of the *Richmodisturm* → p. 68 (photo right): they allude to a saga from the 14th century. Cologne's history after all, is everywhere.

05:00pm SHARP MIND OR TIRED LEGS?

Now you can choose how to spend your afternoon: either relax or see some action in the *Agrippabad* → p. 32, or admire the art treasures in *St Aposteln* → p. 41, one of a dozen important Romanesque churches in Cologne, after you have been inspired by the modern art installations in the *Kölnischer Kunstverein* → p. 40.

07:30pm A TYPICAL COLOGNE EVENING

Feel like hearing some Kölsch spoken? Then you have to get tickets for a traditional puppet show at *Puppenspiele der Stadt Köln* → p. 77 and have a laugh at the comic farces presented. Experience the legendary alternative Cologne scene at *Backes* → p. 75, or end your day at one of Cologne's most elegant cocktail bars *Rosebud* → p. 76.

Starting point: Dom
End point: Dom/Hauptbahnhof
Information: Tourist Service Centre directly opposite the cathedral

SIGHTSEEING

CITY **WHERE TO START?**
Dom (113 E2) (*ℳ G4*): Take the U 5, 16 or 18 to Dom/Hauptbahnhof (main train station) or use the cathedral or the Dom/Rhein car park. Now you are right in the old town and in the shopping area that starts at Wallrafplatz/Hohe Straße. Cross Marzellenstraße and you'll be in the Eigelstein Quarter within 7 minutes and if you cross Hohenzollern Bridge, you'll get to the Rhine embankment within 10 minutes from the cathedral.

Cologne's tourist highlights include Unesco World Heritage sites like the cathedral, its Romanesque churches, as well as the city's many museums and the Rhine waterfront. And of course, there is also the carnival – the Rose Monday parade attracts a remarkable 1.5 million visitors annually.

The majority of tourist attractions are in the city centre and are all easily reached by foot. At the end of the war in 1945, 90 per cent of Cologne's inner city was destroyed. The restoration of the Romanesque churches and the town hall tower to their original state continued up to the end of the 1980s. The tower facade is adorned

Photo: Beer garden with the narrow gabled houses and Groß St Martin

In the shadow of the Dom: where the old and the new, current culture and folklore meet to create a way of life unique to Cologne

with 124 figures representing the city's history from Roman times to the present. In addition to the sites of the old town or Altstadt there is also modern Cologne. After 1980 the Dom/Rhein-Komplex was established with the Museum Ludwig and the Rheingarten. In the western part of the city centre the Mediapark was built in 1990 and today the Rheinauhafen has a new look. However, between the old gates of Eigelsteintor and Severintor there are constant reminders of the city's history from the past 2000 years: Roman excavations, traces of its medieval past and reminders of the early history of its industrial culture.

They bear witness to a proud and self-confident citizenship, to which Cologne also owes its museums. Since the clergyman Ferdinand Franz Wallraf (1748–1824)

The map shows the location of the most interesting districts. There is a detailed map of each district on which each of the sights described is numbered.

saved many ecclesiastical treasures (which would otherwise have been destroyed) during the 1800 secularisation, the citizens of Cologne have been art collectors and art donors.

ALTSTADT

During the Second World War the area around Groß St Martin was completely destroyed. Its subsequent reconstruction was not true to the original: the narrow winding alleys of the Altstadt had already been completely renovated in the 1930s.

In the 1970s city leaders promoted the development of the area as a pub district – as a counterpart to the Altstadt

of Düsseldorf who claimed that they had the 'longest bar in the world'.

■ ALTER MARKT ● ⊰⊱
(113 E3) *(ⅉ G5)*

From the café terraces you will have a lovely view (despite the subway construction work) of the historic town hall, the Jan von Werth Fountain and the colourful medieval houses in the old market. Look up at house number 24 you will see the naked buttocks of the *Kallendresser* – a little figure that is part of the history of Cologne – but tourists can rest assured that the *Kallendresser* will steer clear from their plates when nature calls!

Built in 1884, the fountain has a story behind it: Jan von Werth was a simple farm boy who was rejected by the maid

Griet for not being fine enough. When he returned from the Thirty Years' War a proud cavalry general, Griet (who now was selling flowers at the city gates) regretted not marrying Jan. *U/S-Bahn and buses: Dom/Hauptbahnhof or Heumarkt*

2 ARCHAEOLOGICAL ZONE/ JEWISH MUSEUM ● ♨
(113 E3) *(ØD G5)*

On the square in front of the town hall is a museum for Jewish cultural heritage. This Jewish Museum and the remnants of the Mikveh ritual bath *(→ p. 33)* form part of an archaeological zone that extends as an underground museum for over 33,000 ft² beneath the old town hall and the new ' Spanish' town hall. In addition to the Praetorium *(→ p. 35)*, the portico under the historic town hall *(→ p. 35)*), the Roman sewers beneath Großen Budengasse and the *Ubian Monu-*

ment (Tue–Sun 10am–5pm, first Thu of the month until 10pm, entrance only during tours and for groups, key at the Praetorium's counter | An der Malzmuhle) there is also the corner tower that dates back to the 4th century (the oldest Roman ashlar building north of the Alps) which completes the ensemble. The name of the construction comes from the fact that the Romans founded their colony on the territory of a Germanic tribe, the Ubii.

One may enter the Praetorium, the Mikveh and the Roman sewer at any time, but the excavations under the town hall and the square, may currently only be viewed during special tours. *Main entrance archaeological zone: at the old Ratskeller on the Alter Markt, at time of going to press, still in the planning phase | entrance: 3 euros Praetorium, 1 euro Mikveh and Ubian Monument, combi-ticket Praetorium and Roman-Germanic Museum 8*

MARCO POLO HIGHLIGHTS

euros, free tours Fri 2pm; meeting place: Am Grabungszelt, northern side, opposite the 'Spanish' part of the town hall | tel. 0221 22 13 34 22, group reservations tel. 0221 22 12 23 94| CCAA@stadt-koeln.de| www.museenkoeln.de | U-Bahn and buses: Heumarkt

◼3 DOM ⭐

(113 E2) *(∅ G4)*

The legend of St Gereon and St Ursula established *hillige Köle* (Holy Cologne) as a pilgrim's metropolis during the Middle Ages. In 1164 the purported remains of the Three Wise Men were brought to Cologne from Milan. A shrine was needed for the bones and the resulting medieval masterpiece was completed in 1215 and of course had to be built to house the shrine. The cornerstone was laid in 1248. Master Gerhard, the first cathedral building master, favoured the high-Gothic style of the French churches. But the cathedral was never completed and in 1560 building work was halted due to the plague and the economical decline of the city.

Ironically, the Protestant Prussians completed the cathedral in 1880, claiming it as their political right and making it a national cultural icon. At the time of its completion, the cathedral was the tallest building in the world.

The colourful glass windows bathe the interior of the church in a mystical light and create a spiritual atmosphere. The solid walls are 'dissolved' by large window surfaces and slender traceries. The modern glass windows designed by the artist Gerhard Richter contain more then 11,500 coloured glass squares, INSIDER TIP which are beautiful in the afternoon sun. The

Solemn mass in the light-filled interior of Cologne's cathedral

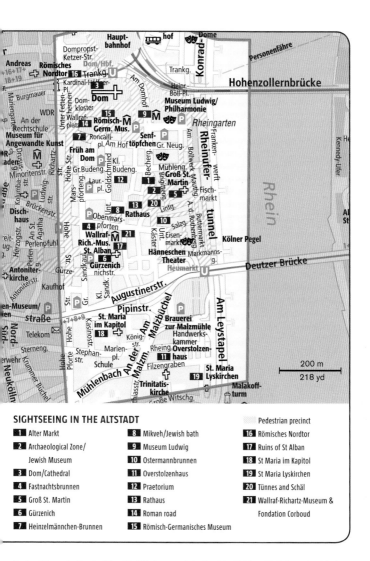

SIGHTSEEING IN THE ALTSTADT

1 Alter Markt

2 Archaeological Zone/
Jewish Museum

3 Dom/Cathedral

4 Fastnachtsbrunnen

5 Groß St. Martin

6 Gürzenich

7 Heinzelmännchen-Brunnen

8 Mikveh/Jewish bath

9 Museum Ludwig

10 Ostermannbrunnen

11 Overstolzenhaus

12 Praetorium

13 Rathaus

14 Roman road

15 Römisch-Germanisches Museum

16 Römisches Nordtor

17 Ruins of St Alban

18 St Maria im Kapitol

19 St Maria Lyskirchen

20 Tünnes and Schäl

21 Wallraf-Richartz-Museum &
Fondation Corboud

░ Pedestrian precinct

Lady of Grace in front of the *Dreikönigen-altar* in the northern transept is often called the 'decorated Madonna' because of all the votive offerings pinned on to her by grateful believers. The wooden pulpit behind one of the pillars of the transept dates back to 1544 and is Cologne's oldest. The archbishop's throne can also be seen in the crossing. The Gero Cross (circa 976) on the northern side of the ambulatory is one of the oldest large-scale statues from the Middle Ages still in existence.

At the end of the aisle is the altar of the patron saints of the city, St Ursula and St Gereon. This altarpiece was originally painted for the town hall chapel by Stefan Lochner. *Nov–April daily 6am–7.30pm, May–Oct daily 6am–9pm | tours Mon–Sat 11am–12.30pm, 2–3.30pm, Sun 2–3.30pm | entrance 5 euros | Multivision in the Cinema Domforum (opposite Westportal): Mon–Sat noon, 1.30pm, 3pm, 4.30pm | entrance 2 euros | www.koelner-dom.de | U/S-Bahn and buses: Dom/Hauptbahnhof* It takes about half an hour to reach the top of the ☆ Dom tower with its 533 stairs. In the iron belfry you can admire the heavy bell which is called *dä decke Pitter* or 'the fat Peter' in Kölsch. When it was cast in Apolda in 1923, it was the heaviest ringable bell in the world, at 24 tons. *March, April, Oct daily 9am–5pm, May–Sept daily 9am–6pm, Nov–Feb daily 9am–4pm | Domkloster 4 | entrance 2.50 euros*

In 1969 a square (the *Domplatte*) designed by the architect Fritz Schaller, was built around the cathedral. In front of the main entrance of the cathedral and on Roncalliplatz at it's southern end, urban life plays itself out: jugglers, pavement artists and the professional demonstrator Walter Herman all vie for attention. At the eastern side however, the *Domplatte* leads to a dark and dreary concrete monstrosity, its demolition has been the subject of discussions for many years.

▮4 FASTNACHTSBRUNNEN
(113 E3) *(𝄪 G5)*

In 1825 Goethe participated in the carnival and then warned against its wild excesses saying, 'a little madness is commendable when it is brief and for a reason ...' This inscription adorns Georg Grassegger's fountain (1913) alongside figures from Cologne's folklore: the *Rote Funken* dressed as city soldiers, the holy virgin and her servants, the oldest dance group of the carnival and a figure in *Kluten* costume, the traditional dress of Rhine harbour workers. *Gülichplatz | www.karneval. de | U-Bahn and buses: Heumarkt*

▮5 GROSS ST MARTIN
(113 E–F3) *(𝄪 G5)*

This basilica was built on the foundations of Roman warehouses. It was consecrated in 1172 but the tower was only finished in 1200. It was the city's most famous landmark until the completion of the cathedral in the 19th century. *Tue–Sat 8.30am–7.30pm, Sun 1–7.15pm | www.romanische-kirchen-koeln.de | Groß St Martin 9 | U/S-Bahn and buses: Dom/Hauptbahnhof* After visiting the church, you can relax in the beer garden at the ★ *Fischmarkt* just a few feet away. Between Groß St Martin

RELAX & ENJOY

At the ● Agrippabad everyone gets their money's worth: children can enjoy the 130 m (426 ft) long tube slide while their parents relax in the saunas or enjoy the beer garden. There is also a lawn and a restaurant. **(112 C5) *(𝄪 F6)*** *Swimming pool 6.30am–10.30pm, Sat/ Sun 9am–9pm, sauna Mon–Fri 9am–11pm, Sat/Sun 9am–9pm, gym Mon–Fri 6.30am–10.30pm, Sat/Sun 9am–8pm | pool 5.40 euros/2.5 hrs, sauna 14 euros/ 2 hrs | Kämmergasse 1 | tel. 0221 279 17 30 | www.koelnbaeder.de | U-Bahn and buses: Neumarkt* and the *Rheingarten* lies the extensive *Stapelhaus* (storehouse): during the Middle Ages all ships travelling on the Rhine, had to drop anchor in Cologne for three days and present all their wares in the *Stapelhaus*. This gave Cologne's tradesmen control of the Rhine trade. *U-Bahn and buses: Heumarkt*

▆6 GÜRZENICH
(113 E3–4) (*ω G5*)

The medieval emperor was crowned 70 km (44 mi) away in Aachen and often stopped over in Cologne. In order to receive him, an impressive ceremonial house was needed, so in 1437, the council decided to build a banqueting and dance hall large enough for 4000 guests. Later on the building served as a warehouse and it was only in the 19th century that it was once again a concert house and ballroom. *Martinstraße 29–31 | U 1, 2, 7, 9: Heumarkt*

▆7 HEINZELMÄNNCHEN-BRUNNEN
(113 E2) (*ω G4*)

This fountain depicts a fairytale by August Kopisch (1836). It describes how during the night hard-working elves did all the work so that the residents of Cologne could be lazy during the day. But, a tailor's wife was curious and wanted to see the elves so one night she scattered peas on her stairs. The elves slipped on the peas and tumbled downstairs and they then disappeared forever. Thereafter, Cologne's inhabitants had to do all their own work. In the symbolism of the fairytale, the sleeping residents represent the medieval city and its century-old structures which remained in place until 1794. It was only when the Napoleonic occupying forces left Cologne in 1800 – leaving behind a modern administration – that the city started a new and modern era of business and economic prosperity. *Am Hof | U/S-Bahn and buses: Dom/Hauptbahnhof*

Cologne's first landmark: the tower of Groß St Martin

▆8 MIKVEH/JEWISH BATH
(113 E3) (*ω G5*)

Cologne's Jewish community dates back to the 4th century and is the oldest north of the Alps. During the Middle Ages the Jews lived in the current Town Hall Quarter. The remains of the Mikveh ritual bath (circa 1150) can be seen on the square. Its water levels depended on the water level of the Rhine. *Key obtainable at the Praetorium with prior arrangement Tue–Sun 10am–5pm, 45 min loan | Unter Goldschmied | U/S-Bahn and buses: Dom/Hauptbahnhof*

Not only the Picasso collection impresses in the Museum Ludwig

9 MUSEUM LUDWIG ★ ●
(113 E2) (*G4*)

The Museum Ludwig is the flagship of Cologne's museums. It houses the city's entire art collection from the 20th and 21st centuries. A collector couple – Peter and Irene Ludwig – donated their collection of Pop Art to the city in 1968. Later Peter Ludwig also brought lesser known avant-garde works from Russia to the Rhine. He remained an active collector right up to the last years of his life (he passed away in 1996) and collected artworks from China and Cuba, that epitomised the idea of Global Art – an expression of the same life experiences of the younger generation of artists, whether they live in Havana, Shanghai, Berlin or New York.

This collector's programme is a permanent exhibition. Thanks to his widow Irene Ludwig, who made a generous donation in 2001, the museum houses the third largest Picasso collection in the world. In the project halls A/C and D/C with its changing exhibitions of contemporary artists, you can also have a look at the work of Expressionists like Ernst Ludwig Kirchner, Max Beckmann and others, as well as works from the Fluxus and Nouveau réalisme movements of the 1960s (Arman, Yves Klein, Daniel Spoerri and others). *Tue–Sun 10am–6pm, first Thu of the month until 10pm | Heinrich-Böll-Platz | entrance 10 euros | www.museum-ludwig. de | U/S-Bahn and buses: Dom/Hauptbahnhof*

10 OSTERMANNBRUNNEN
(113 E3) (*G5*)

Willi Ostermann (1876–1936) wrote more than a hundred patriotic songs and carnival hits which are still popular today. The fountain monument (1938) shows figures from his songs. *Ostermannplatz | U-Bahn and buses: Heumarkt*

11 INSIDER TIP OVERSTOLZENHAUS

(113 E4) (*M G5*)

With its stepped gables, it is the only remaining patrician house in the Romanesque style. The exterior of the 1230 house which belonged to the Overstolz family – wealthy wine merchants – still looks beautiful. The interior though must have been very cold and draughty with its high ceilings. *Rheingasse 8 | buses 132, 133, U 1, 7, 9: Heumarkt*

12 PRAETORIUM (113 E3) (*M G5*)

In 1953 the new 'Spanish' town hall was built opposite the historical town hall. At that point builders found the palace construction of the Roman governors, the praetors. The excavation and sewer system can be viewed in the basement of the new building. It seems like the praetors even splashed out and had the comfort of under floor heating to ward off the cold! *Tue–Sun 10am–5pm | Kleine Budengasse (side entrance of the 'Spanish Building') | entrance 3 euros, combi-ticket with the Roman-Germanic Museum 8 euros | tel. 0221 22 12 23 94 | www.museenkoeln.de |* bus 132: Rathaus | U/S-Bahn and buses: Dom/Hauptbahnhof

13 RATHAUS ⭐

(113 E3) (*M G5*)

In 1414 the 61 m (200 ft) high late-Gothic town hall tower was completed. Representing a visual expression of the self-confidence of the city's citizens, it was built to stand out from the surrounding churches. At the back of the building is a dramatic symbol of citizenship: the 'Platzjabbeck', a carved wooden head that sticks its tongue out every hour. The town hall gallery in the Renaissance style dates back to the year 1573. The interior of the the 'Piazetta' with its 12 m (39 ft) high atrium is freely accessible. From the northern wall you have a view of the tower. *Mon–Tue 9am–3pm, Fri 9–noon | Rathausplatz | bus 132: Rathaus | U/S-Bahn: Dom/Hauptbahnhof*

14 ROMAN ROAD (113 E2) (*M G4*)

The Roman road at the Roman-Germanic Museum was reconstructed using original cobble stones. *Roncalliplatz eastern side | U/S-Bahn and buses: Dom/Hauptbahnhof*

Ostermann's fountain with figures from his most famous songs

15 RÖMISCH-GERMANISCHES MUSEUM ★ (113 E2) (*Ø G4*)

The most valuable exhibition of this Roman-Germanic Museum is the Dionysius mosaic, which came from the dining room of a 4th century Roman villa. Another striking monument is the tomb of the Roman veteran Poblicius (circa 40 AD). Take your time as you view the many interesting archaeological artefacts, which

museenkoeln.de | U/S-Bahn and buses: Dom/Hauptbahnhof

16 RÖMISCHES NORDTOR (113 D2) (*Ø G4*)

The remains of the Roman north gate, a part of the Roman city wall, can be found at the northern end of the cathedral. *Trankgasse/Domplatte | U/S-Bahn and buses: Dom/Hauptbahnhof*

Travel through the city's rich past: Römisch-Germanisches Museum

date back to Cologne's Roman origins. The museum has the world's largest Roman glass collection and the highlight is its diachronic glass cup from the 4th century. The fact that so many jewellery pieces are exhibited, can be explained by the fact that they had a practical function: bracelets and necklaces were used as capital assets and currency. *Tue–Sun 10am–5pm | Roncalliplatz 4 | entrance 6 euros | www.*

17 RUINS OF ST ALBAN (113 E3–4) (*Ø G5*)

Only the ruins are left of this parish church which was destroyed in 1945. A copy of the statue of the *Mourning Parents* by Käthe Kollwitz (1931) was placed in the ruins, which serves as a memorial to those who died during the Second World War. *Quatermarkt 4 | U 1, 7, 8, 9: Heumarkt*

🔢 ST MARIA IM KAPITOL
(113 E4) (*🗺 G5*)

Based on the Church of Nativity in Bethlehem, the building was consecrated in 1065 and its mixture of central and 'long house' basilica elements make it unique. An unusual curiosity is the Pleistocene era whale bones which the locals call *Zint Märjens Rip* (St Maria's ribs). *Daily 10am–6pm | Kasinostraße 6 | www.romanische-kirchen-koeln.de | U-Bahn and buses: Heumarkt*

🔢 ST MARIA LYSKIRCHEN
(113 E5) (*🗺 G5–6*)

A visit to this church, which was first mentioned in a document in 984, is a must for its 2 m (6 ft) high wooden figure of the 'Seaman's Madonna' (circa 1420) and its beautiful dome and wall paintings depicting biblical scenes. *Daily 10am–6pm | An Lyskirchen 8 | www.romanische-kirchen-koeln.de | U-Bahn and buses: Heumarkt*

🔢 TÜNNES AND SCHÄL
(113 E3) (*🗺 G5*)

One of Cologne's great characters Jupp Engel, commissioned sculptor Ewald Mataré to create the Tünnes and Schäl Monument, the two legendary puppet characters are still very much a part of Cologne's everyday culture and humour. Engels also donated the adjacent Schmitz Column. *Brigittengässchen | U/S-Bahn and buses: Dom/Hauptbahnhof*

🔢 WALLRAF-RICHARTZ-MUSEUM & FONDATION CORBOUD ⭐
(113 E3) (*🗺 G5*)

This museum houses art from the medieval period through to 19th century Impressionism. The art is grouped according to era. Gothic panel paintings, which mainly depict religious themes, form a magnificent golden backdrop. In the sec-

tion of the old Dutch masters, one can see how secular themes became popular during the 15th and 16th century: still lifes with gleaming tableware, pubs and market scenes, views of Dutch parlours and – the highlight – a self-portrait by Rembrandt (1668).

A viewing of the Romantic and Biedermeier Realism painters of the 19th century is also highly recommended. Painters of these movements were Caspar David Friedrich, Josef Anton Koch, Ferdinand Georg Waldmüller and Carl Spitzweg. Have a look at the works of Impressionists, from Claude Monet to Lovis Corinth and others. *Tue, Wed, Fri 10am–6pm, Thu 10am–10pm Sat/Sun 11am–6pm | Martinstraße 39 | entrance 7 euros, combi-ticket with special exhibitions 9 euros | www.museenkoeln.de | U/S-Bahn and buses: Dom/Hauptbahnhof or Heumarkt*

LOW BUDGET

▶ Entrance to the ● *Kölner Dommusik* concerts at the shrine of the Three Wise Men is free, as are the organ concerts that take place every Tuesday at 8pm from June until September. At the end of the concert, a donation is requested. *www.koelner-dommusik.de*

▶ Entrance is also free at the *Stattmuseum Köln-Sülz*. The artists' association Akt 1 e.V. organises exhibitions of young up-and-coming artists. The art is already museum-worthy hence the 'museum'in the title *(118 C2) (🗺 D7) Thu/Fri 3–7pm, Sat noon–3pm | Gustavstraße 11 | tel. 0221 3 10 01 82 | www.koelnsalon-akteins.de | U 9 Lindenburg*

CENTRE

'I am going to the city,' is what the old hands of Nippes and Ehrenfeld still say, when they go shopping in the city centre. 'Centre' here means the medieval part of Cologne between the Rhine and Ringen. The district is divided in a cross shape: the Roman Heerstraße from Bonn to Neuss runs between the Eigelstein Gate and the Severins Gate, from north to south while Hahnestraße, Neumarkt and Schildergasse form the east-west axis. During the Middle Ages, the Schildergasse was home to the city's signwriters.

■1 ANTONITERKIRCHE

(113 D4) (*M* F5)

This Gothic style church was built in 1384 and in 1802, at Napoleon I's behest, was given to the Protestants as their first church in Cologne. Ernst Barlach's *Schwebender Engel* (Floating Angel) can be seen in the northern recess, which serves as a memorial to those who died during the World Wars. *Mon–Fri 11am–7.30pm, Sat 11am–5pm, Sun 9.30am–7pm | Schildergasse 57 | www.antonitercitykirche.de | U-bahn and buses: Neumarkt*

■2 EHRENSTRASSE

(112 B3) (*M* E–F5)

Even though its small quirky boutiques have given way to large chain stores recently, Ehrenstraße still remains very hip and modern with numerous trendy bistros. A see-and-be-see ritual plays itself out on Saturdays. Need to get your breath back? Where Ehrenstraße, Apostelnstraße and Breite Straße meet, the outdoor restaurants on Willy Millowitsch Square will be your best bet. **INSIDER TIP** Motorists beware: cyclists are allowed to use the one-way street in both directions. *U-Bahn and buses: Neumarkt/Rudolfplatz/Friesenplatz*

For boutiques and bistros take a stroll along trendy Ehrenstraße

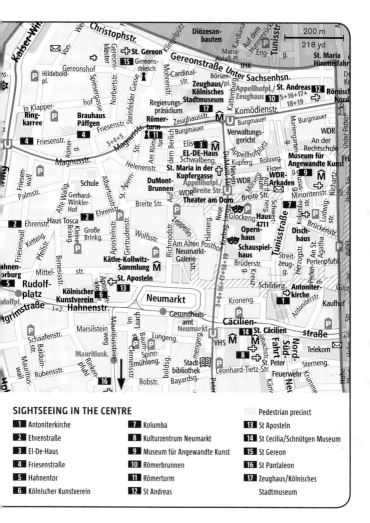

SIGHTSEEING IN THE CENTRE

3 INSIDER TIP EL-DE-HAUS

(112 C2) (*ⓜ F4*)

This cellar with its prison cells is one of the most terrible places in the city: during the Nazi reign, the Gestapo tortured prisoners here. Inscriptions on the walls document the prisoner's suffering. The permanent exhibition about Cologne during the Nazi reign is supplemented by special exhibitions on the topic. *Tue–Fri 10am–4pm, Sat/Sun 11am–4pm | Appellhofplatz 23–25 | entrance 4.20 euros, tours by appointment (only closed groups) see website, bookings essential tel: 0221 22 12 63 31 | www.museenkoeln.de/ns-dok | U-Bahn and buses: Appellhofplatz*

4 FRIESENSTRASSE (112 B2) (*ⓜ E4*)

Tourists from the countryside flock to Klein Köln (Little Cologne) on weekends, but despite this influx its many cocktail bars stay hip and happening. All kinds of international gastronomy can be found here, from a Kölsch brewery pub, to sushi stalls, Spanish tapas or Irish pubs. And, on summer evenings, people even party in the middle of the street. *U-Bahn and buses: Friesenplatz*

cinema. *Tue–Fri 1–7pm, Sat/Sun 11am–6pm | Hahnenstraße 6 | entrance 4 euros | tel. 0221 21 70 21 | www.koelnischerkunst verein.de | U-Bahn and buses: Neumarkt*

7 INSIDER TIP KOLUMBA (113 D3) (*ⓜ F5*)

This former Diocese Museum now houses modern and contemporary art. The permanent exhibition is changed annually on the 14th of September (Holy Cross Day).

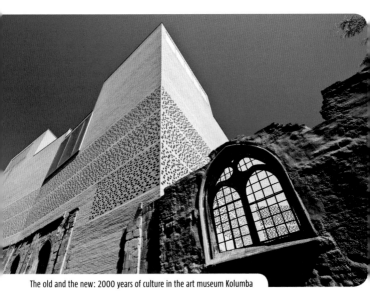

The old and the new: 2000 years of culture in the art museum Kolumba

5 HAHNENTOR (112 A4) (*ⓜ E5*)

Along with the Eigelsteintor and Severinstor, the Hahnentor – a typical double tower gate – is the third of the city's medieval gates. *Rudolplatz/An d'r Hahnepooz | U-Bahn and buses: Rudolfplatz*

6 KÖLNISCHER KUNSTVEREIN (112 B4) (*ⓜ E5*)

The art association exhibits young artist's experimental art installations. Film programmes are also often shown in its

Fri–Wed noon–5pm | Kolumbastraße 2–4 | www.kolumba.de | U/S-Bahn and buses: Dom/Hauptbahnhof

8 KULTURZENTRUM NEUMARKT ● (112 C4) (*ⓜ F5*)

This building, completed in 2010, houses three different museums: the Schnütgen Museum of religious art, the Rautenstrauch-Joest Museum for world culture and the JuniorMuseum. All three museums share a communal library.

A glass covered passage connects the *Schnütgen Museum* with its other rooms in the neighbouring St Cecilia church. The collection of religious art includes wonderful wood and stone sculptures, precious medieval carved altarpieces, textiles, fine gold, silver and bronze metalwork, ivory carvings, stained glass windows, Roman and Gothic sculptures and large church furniture.

At first sight the INSIDER TIP ▸ *Rautenstrauch-Joest Museum* looks like a 7 m (22 ft) high Indonesian rice barn. Its exhibitions are not arranged according to region of origin, but according to themes such as 'Homes', 'Religion' and 'Stereotypes and Prejudice'. A separate part of the museum, the *Junior-Museum,* shows five different children's rooms from various cultures and documents coming-of-age rituals. *Tue–Sun 10am–6pm, Thu 10am–8pm | entrance Rautenstrauch-Joest-Museum 6 euros, JuniorMuseum free thereafter, Schnütgen Museum 5 euros, combi-ticket Schnütgen/ Rautenstrauch 9 euros | Cäcilienstraße 29–33 | www.museenkoeln.de | U-Bahn and buses: Neumarkt*

9 MUSEUM FÜR ANGEWANDTE KUNST (113 D2) (*Ø F4–5*)
A well presented collection of applied art and design from different eras, ranging from medieval to the present. The collection showcases art nouveau porcelain, wedding garments from the 1930s, as well as furniture, pewter and television sets. *Tue–Sun 11am–5pm, first Thu of the month until 10pm, tours Wed 11am, Sat/ Sun 2.30pm | An der Rechtschule | entrance 6 euros | www.museenkoeln.de | U/S-Bahn and buses: Dom/Hauptbahnhof*

10 RÖMERBRUNNEN
(112–113 C–D2) (*Ø F4*)
Franz Brantzky created this fountain in 1915 with its she-wolf and relief panel depicting themes from Roman history. *Between Burgmauer and Komödienstraße | U-Bahn and buses: Appellhofplatz*

11 RÖMERTURM
(114 B–C2) (*Ø F4*)
The corner tower of the Roman city wall with its mosaic from natural stone dates back to AD 50. *St Apernstraße/Zeughausstraße | U-Bahn and buses: Appellhofplatz*

12 ST ANDREAS
(113 D2) (*Ø F4*)
This striking building in late Romanesque (approx. 1200) style has a Gothic chancel which was only finished in 1492. The scientist, friar and theologian Albertus Magnus (approx. 1200–80) is interred in its crypt. *Mon–Fri 7am–7pm, Sat/Sun 8am–7pm | Komödienstraße 4–8 | www.romanische-kirchen-koeln.de | U/S-Bahn and buses: Dom/Hauptbahnhof*

13 ST APOSTELN
(112 B3–4) (*Ø E5*)
Late Romanesque building (approx. 1030) with a 66 m (217 ft) high tower. Ludwig Gies decorated the windows of the chapel that was added in 1956. Gies also designed the famous *Bundesadler* sculpture for the Bonn Bundestag. The *Adenauer Memorial* is found at the northern side of the church. From 1917–33 and for a few months during 1945, Konrad Adenauer was Cologne's Lord Mayor and from 1949–63 he was the Chancellor of Germany. *Wed–Mon 10am–noon and 3–5pm | Apostelnkloster 10 | www.romanische-kirchen-koeln.de | U-Bahn and buses: Neumarkt*

14 ST CECILIA/ SCHNÜTGEN MUSEUM
(112 113 C–D4) (*Ø F5*)
The twin churches of St Peter and St Cecilia make for a remarkable sight. The

Impressive Romanesque church with Roman masonry: St Gereon

new Schnütgen Museum displays a wide selection of religious art although St Cecilia's remains home to its medieval collection. *(Further information → p. 41) Tue–Sun 10am–6pm, Thu 10am–8pm | entrance 6 euros, combi-ticket Schnütgen/Rautenstrauch Museum 9 euros | Cäcilienstraße 29–33 | www.romanische-kirchen-koeln. de, www.museenkoeln.de | U-Bahn and buses: Neumarkt*

15 INSIDER TIP ST GEREON
(112 B–C1) (*M F4*)

The Roman officer Gereon was the captain of the Theban legionnaires who was said to have died a martyr's death here. In 1191 building of this Romanesque church

was completed. The baptistery and the southern sacristy date back to the 13–14th century. The original Roman interior walls (still visible) are 16 m (53 ft) high. Special highlight: the floor mosaic depicting scenes from the lives of David and Samson. *Mon–Sat 10am–6pm, Sun 12.30–6pm | Gereonsdriesch 4 | www. romanische-kirchen-koeln.de | U-Bahn: Christophstraße/Mediapark*

16 ST PANTALEON (112 C6) (*M F6*)

The oldest Romanesque church in Cologne (probably pre-1002) is the burial church of the Archbishop Bruno and the Empress Theophanu. The Ottonian single-nave church was extended to a three-aisled

DEUTZ

The exhibition centre, the Lanxess Arena, the administrative town hall, the Köln Triangle and the newly built hotels all form part of the architectural landscape of this district.

In the year 310 the Romans installed a wooden pontoon bridge – where the Deutzer Bridge is today – which was protected by the Divitia fort on the right Rhine bank. Visit the other side of the Rhine bank: ● ⚲ from the Deutz side, you will have a great view of the cathedral and the old town.

■ INSIDER TIP COLOGNE BEACH CLUB KM 689 ● ⚲ (116 C4) (*ᗰ H4*)

In the words of the Kölsch band Paveier, 'The only beach with a view of the Dom'. Relax on the soft sand and you'll feel as if you really are at the beach. Entrance and loungers are free when purchases of at least 4 euros are made. *May to Sept daily noon–1am | Rheinpark | free entrance | www.km689.rhein-terrassen.de | U/S-Bahn and buses: Deutz/Messe*

■ KÖLN TRIANGLE ⚲ (116 C4) (*ᗰ H4*)

Getting up to the 28th floor only takes half a minute! Then a further 29 steps take you up to the viewing platform at 103 m (337 ft). On a clear day there are breathtaking views of the city as well as the distant mountain peaks. *Oct–April, Mon–Fri noon–6pm, Sat/Sun 10am–6pm, May–Sept Mon–Fri 11am–10pm, Sat/Sun 10am–10pm | Ottoplatz 1 | entrance 3 euros | www.koeln-triangle.de | U/S-Bahn and buses: Deutz/Messe*

■ LANXESS ARENA (117 D5) (*ᗰ J5*)

Germany's largest indoor arena for sporting events, shows and concerts. *Willy-Brandt-*

basilica with three towers in 1152. *Mon–Fri 9am–6pm, Sat 9am–4pm, and Sun noon–6 pm | Am Pantaleonsberg 12 | www.romanische-kirchen-koeln.de | U-Bahn and buses: Poststraße*

■ ZEUGHAUS/KÖLNISCHES STADTMUSEUM (112 C2) (*ᗰ F4*)

This building was built around 1600 as the city's armoury and weapons arsenal. Today, as the city museum, it documents the history of Cologne since medieval times. The golden *Flügelauto*, a sculpture by HA Schult (1989), stands on top of the tower. *Tue 10am–8pm, Wed–Sun 10am–5pm | Zeughausstraße 1–3 | entrance 5 euros | U-Bahn and buses: Appellhofplatz*

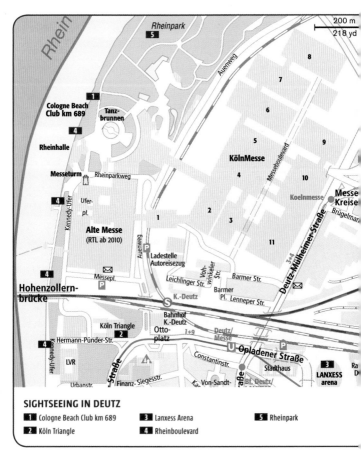

SIGHTSEEING IN DEUTZ

1 Cologne Beach Club km 689
2 Köln Triangle
3 Lanxess Arena
4 Rheinboulevard
5 Rheinpark

Platz 3 | Ticket Hotline tel. 0221 80 20 or 28 01 | www.lanxess-arena.de | U 1, 3, 4, 8, 9 Deutz/Kölnarena

4 RHEINBOULEVARD
(116 C4–6) (ℳ H4–6)
By the year 2016 the Deutzer Rhine bank (between the Rheinpark, the Poller Wiesen and behind the Severins Bridge) will have a new look. A 'media shore' will replace the old exhibition halls and will merge into a new boulevard with a recreation

waterfront at its southern end. *Kennedy-Ufer* | U/S-Bahn and buses: Deutz/Messe

5 RHEINPARK
(116 C3–4) (ℳ H3–4)
This riverside park was enlarged to its current form after the German Garden Show was hosted here in 1957. Locals meet at the INSIDER TIP *Rheinterrassen* and at the neighbouring *Cologne Beach Club km 689*. The ● *Claudius-Therme* with its warm 30° C (86° F) water is at the northern end

of the park. From here, you can take a trip to the Zoo on the opposite side by cable car. *Cable car mid March to beginning of Nov daily 10am–6pm | 4 euros | www.koelner-seilbahn.de | U/S-Bahn and buses: Deutz/Messe*

EIGELSTEIN QUARTER

Kölsch and kebabs, pubs and gourmet restaurants, breweries and bistros: all thrive side by side in this colourful district.
The rather bleak areas around its railway embankment have been used as locations for the popular German *Tatort* television series.

■ BASTEI (116 B3) (*M G–H3*)

The Bastei was built as a Prussian fortification in 1891 in front of the medieval city wall (demolished in 1880). It was rebuilt in 1927 and has a rotunda that juts 8 m (26 ft) over the Rhine. *Konrad-Adenauer-Ufer 80 | U-Bahn and buses: Breslauer Platz*

■ EIGELSTEINTORBURG ★
(116 A3) (*M G3*)
The city gate in the direction of Neuss was called the 'Adlerpforte' but after the French occupation (1794–1814) was renamed 'Eigel' a phonetic Germanisation of the French term *porte d'aigle*. Those who donated their wedding rings to melt down during the First World War, were allowed to hammer a nail into the statue of the *Kölsche Boor* (Cologne farmer) which represents the valour of the city. A relief of this medieval farmer can be seen on the left tower. Later, the inscription was reinterpreted as a symbol of loyalty towards the Empire. It loosely translates as, 'Hold on to the Kingdom, farmer, let it not fall,

be the times sweet or sour'. The remains of a wooden rescue boat hangs in an alcove of the right tower, in memory of those who died in the *MS Cölln* during the First World War. *Eigelstein | U-Bahn and buses: Ebertplatz*

■ GEREONSMÜHLENTURM
(115 E4) (*M F4*)
An original piece of the medieval city wall stands in this section of the Gereonswall. The mill tower is used as a venue for parties. *Gereonswall | U/S-Bahn and buses: Hansaring*

■ ST KUNIBERT (116 B3) (*M G4*)

In 620 Kunibert was elected the Bishop of Cologne. This church which was consecrated in 1247 is the last of the ensemble of churches built in the Romanesque style. *Mon–Sat 10am–1pm and 3–6pm | Kunibert-kloster 6 | www.romanische-kirchen-koeln.de | U-Bahn and buses: Breslauer Platz*

Memories of past conflicts: the medieval fortified Eigelsteintorburg

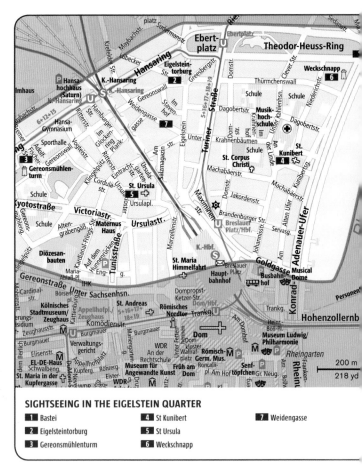

SIGHTSEEING IN THE EIGELSTEIN QUARTER

1 Bastei
2 Eigelsteintorburg
3 Gereonsmühlenturm

4 St Kunibert
5 St Ursula
6 Weckschnapp

7 Weidengasse

5 **ST URSULA** ⭐ (115 F4) (*ω F4*)
The eleven black flames on Cologne's coat of arms represent the British princess Ursula and her following of 11,000 maidens. According to legend, they were all massacred when the Huns besieged Cologne. The Holy St Ursula's remains and other relics are kept in the Golden Chamber. After a rather turbulent time – in terms of finances – a new organ was inaugurated in 2011. *Viewing of the Golden*

Chamber daily upon arrangement: tel. 0221 13 34 00 | Mon–Sat 9am–noon and 3–5pm | www.romanische-kirchen-koeln. de | Ursulaplatz 24 | U/S-Bahn and buses: Dom/Hauptbahnhof

6 **WECKSCHNAPP**
(116 B3) (*ω G3*)
During the Middle Ages this tower served as a prison. When the inmates were desperate for something to eat, they were

tricked into jumping towards a piece of bread *(Weck)* which triggered a trapdoor that lead to their death. *Konrad-Adenauer-Ufer | www.giselmut.de/die_weckschnapp.htm | U-Bahn and buses: Ebertplatz*

7 INSIDER TIP WEIDENGASSE
(116 A3) (*∅ F3*)

This lively and colourful array of junk shops, oriental green grocers, butchers and snack bars is an absolute must! *U-Bahn and buses: Ebertplatz*

SEVERINS QUARTER/ SÜDSTADT

BAP *Kölsch rocker* Wolfgang Niedecken calls this part of the city home. It houses an eclectic mix of people from different social circles: aging ex-squatters, alternative academics, artists, poets, working-class families and Turkish green-grocers.

A quarter filled with history: the pub *Früh em Veedel* is referred to as the 'church of the invalids' in Kölsch because veterans from the First World War used to meet here. For an unadulterated and authentic street carnival experience you should spend INSIDER TIP Weiberfastnacht at the square *An der Eiche* (120 A–B 1–2) (*∅ G7*) or just a block away, the *Severinskirchplatz* (120 B2) (*∅ G7*).

1 BAYENTURM (120 B2) (*∅ G7*)

This tower with its octagonal Gothic upper floors was the starting point of the medieval city wall which was built in a semicircle around the northern part of the city up to the Weckschnapp. Today this building is used as a media, information and document centre for the history of women's emancipation. *Am Bayenturm | www.frauen mediaturm.de | U 6, 15, 17: Ubierring*

Beautifully decorated relics in the Golden Chamber of St Ursula

2 BOTTMÜHLE (120 B2) (⊠ G7)

Built in 1587 this tower served as a grape mill. The quality of the wine that was made then left much to be desired: it was described as *suure Hungk* (sour dog). *Severinswall | U 6, 15, 17: Ubierring*

The Olympic rings show the way: Sport & Olympia Museum

3 DEUTSCHES SPORT & OLYMPIA MUSEUM (113 F5) (⊠ G6)

These exhibitions contain interesting pieces such as the tennis raquet that Boris Becker destroyed and the shoes belonging to Formula 1 champion Michael Schumacher. You can also do various sports here: there is a punch bag for boxers, ride a bicycle in a wind tunnel or play soccer on the roof of INSIDER TIP Cologne's highest soccer pitch. *Tue–Fri 10am–6pm, Sat/ Sun 11am–7pm | Rheinauhafen 1 | entrance 6 euros | group tours tel. 0221 33 60 90 |* www.sportmuseum.de | U 1, 2, 7, 9: Heumarkt, U 3, 4: Severinstraße

4 INSIDER TIP RHEINAUHAFEN (113 F5–6) (⊠ G6)

Only a tiny yacht harbour remains of what was once a Prussian excise port. The area is now characterised by museums, galleries and other businesses unrelated to its maritime past. The beer garden at *Hafenterrasse am Malakoffturm* (1855) has a ☼ beautiful view of the old swing bridge and the Chocolate Museum. *Holzmarkt | buses 132, 133, U 3, 4: Severinstraße*

5 SCHOKOLADENMUSEUM (113 F5) (⊠ G6)

The Imhoff Chocolate Museum, houses one of the world's most unique collections about the history and culture of cocoa plantations and the industrial processing of chocolate. Afterwards you treat yourself in the museum's sweet shop. *Tue–Fri 10am–6pm, Sun 11am–7pm | Rheinauhafen 1a | entrance 7.50 euros | www.schokoladenmuseum.de | bus 106: Schokoladenmuseum, U 1, 7, 9: Heumarkt, U 3, 4: Severinstraße*

6 SEVERINSTORBURG (120 B2) (⊠ G7)

Also serving as a wedding venue, this is the southern counterpart of the Eigelsteintor. On Fat Thursday at about 1.30pm, *'Dat Spill vun Jan un Griet'* – a play about the Cavalry General Jan von Werth – is performed here. *Chlodwigplatz | U-Bahn and buses: Chlodwigplatz*

7 ST GEORG (113 D5) (⊠ F–G6)

INSIDER TIP The only remaining Romanesque pillared basilica in the Rhineland (11th century). Main attraction: the replicas of the Georg and Gabel crucifixes dating back to the 14th century. *Daily 8am–6pm |*

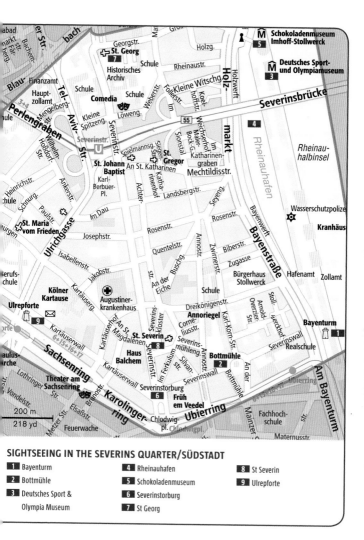

SIGHTSEEING IN THE SEVERINS QUARTER/SÜDSTADT

1 Bayenturm	**4** Rheinauhafen	**8** St Severin
2 Bottmühle	**5** Schokoladenmuseum	**9** Ulrepforte
3 Deutsches Sport & Olympia Museum	**6** Severinstorburg	
	7 St Georg	

Georgsplatz 17 | www.romanische-kirchen-koeln.de | U 3, 4: Severinstraße

8 ST SEVERIN
(120 A2) (Ø G7)

The building of this church during the 4th century, is ascribed to the Saint Severin,

the third bishop of Cologne. The extensions which were finished in 948, were redesigned during the 14th and 15th century. *Mon–Sat 9am–6pm, Sun 9am–noon and 3–5.30pm | Im Ferkulum 29 | www.romanische-kirchen-koeln.de | U-Bahn and buses: Chlodwigplatz*

9 ULREPFORTE
(119 F2) (*ØD F7*)

A section of the original medieval city wall is still intact here. The Ulrepforte and the neighbouring Sachsenturm are used today as the seat of the carnival associations. On the wall is a relief panel which was installed in 1360 and is considered to be the oldest secular monument in Germany. The inscription recalls the defence of an attack launched by the Archbishop against Cologne's civilians in 1268. *Sachsenring | U-Bahn and buses: Ulrepforte*

MORE SIGHTS

BELGISCHES VIERTEL
(115 D5–6) (*ØD D–E 4–5*)

In 1890 the Belgian Quarter was built as a new city district beyond the Ring. Since the 1980s this neighbourhood has become a hub for galleries, bars and late night cafés. The majority of social happenings occur in Aachener Straße. *U-Bahn and buses: Friesenplatz or Rudolfplatz*

BOTANISCHER GARTEN/FLORA ●
(116 C1–2) (*ØD H1–2*)

All around the Flora Ballroom and fountains are masses of exotic and indigenous plants. *Garden: 8am until dusk, greenhouses: Oct–March 10am–4pm, April–Sept 10am–6pm | free entrance | Amsterdamer Straße 34 | www.stadt-koeln.de/6/gruen/flora | bus 134, U 15, 16: Zoo/Flora*

INSIDER TIP ▶ EHRENFELD
(114 B–C 2–5) (*ØD C–D 3–4*)

This former working-class and industrial area is now a creative and design hub that is home to artists, creatives and designers. At the centre of the avant-garde scene is Sabine Voggenreiter's *DQE-Halle (Heliosstraße 35–37)*. In *Körner Straße* you will find all sorts of art, kitsch, fashion jewellery and more. The shops here have names like *Geschmackssachen (no. 56)*, *Wohnzimmer (Living Room) (no. 32)*, *Duck and Cover (no. 73)* or *Utensil (no. 21)*. Organic and healthy fare is served at ☺ *Café Sehnsucht (no. 67)*, and for a bite to eat in the evening try *Simrock Bar (no. 65)*. *www.d-q-e.net | U 3,4: Körner Straße*

INSIDER TIP ▶ MELATEN CEMETERY
(114 B–C4–5) (*ØD G4–5*)

In the past non-Catholics and those who died as a result of epidemics or 'maladies' like the plague were buried outside of the city. After 1810 Melaten became the main cemetery and it is the final resting place for many of Cologne's famous citizens. The beautiful tombs and graves from the 19th century are worth a visit. *March–Oct*

KEEP FIT!

North of the Machabäerstraße junction **(116 B4)** (*ØD G4*) you can jog on the Rhine promenade for about 4 km (2.4 mi) to the Mülheimer Bridge, past the Bastei and underneath the Zoo Bridge. You will have a lovely view of the river and the Rheinpark on the opposite side. Skaters meet at the Süd Bridge at the *Kap 686 Skaterpark* **(120 B3)** (*ØD H8*) for ramps, jumps and tricks. *(Kap am Südkai | U 18: Schönhauser Straße)*.

The architecture says it all: trends are set in the Media Park in Ehrenfeld

7am–8pm, Nov–Feb 8am–5pm | Aachener Straße 204 | bus 963, U 1, 2: Melaten

FRIESENVIERTEL (112 B2–3) *(𝄢 E4)*

This was the corporate base of the Gerling insurance group between 1945–53. Less than a block away in Friedenstraße, the red-light district dominated until the 1980s, but today you will only find trendy cocktail bars, bistros and sushi-stands. *U-Bahn and buses: Friesenplatz*

GEO-MUSEUM ●
(119 D1) *(𝄢 D6)*

The Institute of Mineralogy and Geochemistry of the University of Cologne, presents an extended programme at the newly built library. View their exhibit on the history of life on earth – from the Big Bang up to the present – and they also have a mineralogical display. *Wed 2–8pm, every last Sun of the month 2–5pm | Zülpicher Straße 49 b | Lecture Hall Wing of the Institute of Geoscience | www.geomuseum.uni-koeln.de | U 8, 9: Universität or Dasselstraße/Bahnhof Süd.*

KÖLNER KARNEVALSMUSEUM
(114 A4) *(𝄢 A4)*

Germany's largest museum dedicated to the traditions and customs of the carnival. The history of the revellers is shown here in a space of 15,000 ft² from antiquity up to the present. *Thu 10am–8pm, Fri 10am–5pm, Sat/Sun 11am–5pm | Maarweg 123–126 | entrance 4 euros | tel. 0221 57 40 00 | www.kk-museum.de | U 1: Maarweg*

MUSEUM FÜR OSTASIATISCHE KUNST
(114–115 C–D5) *(𝄢 D5)*

You should definitely visit the cafeteria of the Museum of East Asian Art: the 🌿 terrace offers an impressive view of the Japanese sculptor Masayuki Nagare's stone creation *Kaze no Hata* (Flag in the Wind). Inside this unique museum you will find treasures from the Far East – China, Korea and Japan – and valuable Chinese religious sculptures, Korean ceramics and Japanese priest figurines made from cypress wood. INSIDER TIP The Guardian from the Han Dynasty (12th century) is one of the few remaining fig-

Time out on the river: *Alte Liebe* is a popular boathouse restaurant in Rödenkirchen

ures of this art. *Tue–Sun 11am–5pm, Thu 11am–8pm | Universitätsstraße 100 | entrance 5 euros | www.museenkoeln.de | buses 137, 961, 962, 963, 970, U 1, 2: Universitätsstraße/Aachener Weiher*

PHOTOGRAFISCHE SAMMLUNG DER SK STIFTUNG KULTUR (115 E3) *(ɰ E3)*

On display here are the 1920–30s photographs of people in their social environments taken by August Sander. Other exhibits include the industrial photography of Bernd and Hilla Becher and works by Karl Blossfeldt and Albert Renger-Patzsch. The collection has grown continuously over the past 15 years and today contains examples of most photographic artists important to art history.

The same building houses the *Deutsches Tanzarchiv Köln* (German Dance Archives Cologne) which depicts the history of dance in posters, prints and photos. *Thu–Tue 2–7pm | Im Mediapark 7 | entrance 4.50 euros, combi-ticket with Tanzarchiv 6 euros, Mon free entrance | www.sk-kultur.de | U 6, 15, 17, 19: Christophstraße/Mediapark*

RING

(115–116 E–B 6–2) *(ɰ G3–7)*

After the demolition of the medieval city fortification, the new boulevard was modelled on Vienna's Ringstraße, a semi-circle that encloses the inner city. A popular route to stroll along is the area between Rudolfplatz and Gereonshof which is lined with cafés and bistros. *U 6, 15, 17, 19: Friesen- or Rudolfplatz*

RODENKIRCHEN

(121 E–F6) *(ɰ 0)*

This town is a favourite excursion destination for its picturesque chapel, café terraces, houseboat restaurants, river beach and promenade. The boat trip from the Konrad-Adenauer-Ufer takes half an hour. *One way ticket 4 euros, return ticket 7.30 euros | www.koelntourist.net | U 16: Rodenkirchen*

SKULPTURENPARK ★ ●

(116 C2) *(ɰ H2)*

Every two years, this collection is replaced with 30 new sculptures by contemporary artists like Tony Cragg, Louise Bourgeois, Martin Kippenberger, Martin Willing or Markus Lüpertz. A successful mixture of abstract and figurative work. *April–Sept 10.30am–7pm, Oct–March 10.30am–5pm | Riehler Straße/near Zoobrücke | free entrance | skulpturenparkkoeln.de | U 15, 16: Zoo/Flora*

THEATERMUSEUM
(0) (*III 0*)

See scenery designs, stage pieces, curtains, posters and photos in this huge collection of the Institute of Theatre Science of the University of Cologne. *Viewing by appointment only tel. 02203 60 09 20 | Schloss Wahn | www.schloss-wahn.de | S 12: Porz-Wahn*

ZOOLOGISCHER GARTEN ★
(116 C1–2) (*III H–J 1–2*)

About 7000 animals are kept in the open air enclosures and animal houses at the Cologne Zoo. The INSIDER TIP Regenwaldhaus (rainforest house) is a special attraction with its new enclosure for Thai elephants, as well as the Hippodom with hippos and crocodiles. *Summer daily 9am–6pm, winter daily 9am–5pm | Aquarium 9am–6pm | Riehler Straße 173 | entrance 14 euros | www.koelnerzoo.de | bus 135, U 15, 16: Zoo/Flora*

FURTHER AFIELD

AHR THERMEN ●
(122 C3) (*III 0*)

Recuperate with an exursion to Ahr – the most northerly red wine region in Germany – and go swimming, do water gymnastics, aquarobics or just relax in the sauna. The vulcanic water is 31–36° C (88–97° F) warm. *Sun–Thu 9am–11pm,* *Fri/Sat 9am–midnight | Felix-Rütten-Straße 3 | Bad Neuenahr | two-hour ticket 10–12 euros | www.ahr-thermen.de | train: Bad Neuenahr*

MAX-ERNST-MUSEUM BRÜHL
(122 C3) (*III 0*)

The museum has a large collection of prints and sculptures by the surrealist Max Ernst who was from Brühl (1891–1976). *Tue–Sun 11am–6pm, first Thu of the month until 9pm | Comesstraße 42 | entrance 5 euros | tel. 02234 99 21 5 55 | www.maxernst museum.lvr.de | train: Bahnhof. Brühl*

PHANTASIALAND BRÜHL
(122 C3) (*III 0*)

This theme park is one of the largest and best of its type in Europe with new attractions added every year. *April–Oct daily 9am–6pm, cashier closes 4pm | Berggeiststraße 31–41 | Brühl | day ticket 37.50 euros*

SCHLOSS AUGUSTUSBURG
(122 C3) (*III 0*)

Rhine Prince Clemens August felt that the splendid architecture for which King Louis XIV was famous for was also befitting for him so he had his old moated castle transformed into a magnificent summer palace in the French style. In historical terms, the Baroque staircase designed by Balthasar Neumann, is a highlight.

After a 30 minute walk along the beautiful avenue of linden trees, you reach the hunting lodge *Jagdschlösschen Falkenlust*, where the prince secretly met his lovers. *Feb–Nov Tue–Fri 9am–noon and 1.30–4pm, Sat/Sun 10am–5pm | Schlossstraße 6 | Brühl | entrance 5 euros, Schloss Falkenlust entrance 3.50 euros | tel. 02232 440 00 | www.schlossbruehl.de | train: Brühl-Bahnhof or U 18: Brühl-Mitte and 10 min by foot; with a car: B 51 Brühler Straße/ Brühler Landstraße, in Brühl: signposts Parkplätze (parking).*

FOOD & DRINK

Would you like to try the local cuisine? Then you have to visit a typical Cologne *Brauhaus,* or brewery pub, where you will be served hearty Rhineland cuisine. Of course, in Cologne you can travel all around the culinary world. But this trip must include the local specialities like the famous *Halve Hahn* (half a chicken). The origin of this expression dates back to 18 April 1874 in the Brauhaus Lölgen (which no longer exists) a certain Wilhelm Vierkötter jokingly promised his guests half a chicken for dinner but he served them cheese and bread instead. In the taverns the waiters are called *Köbes*, the Kölsch name for Jacob. Originally they were young

men who assisted with beer sales. They are notorious for their witty humour. If you order a mineral water, he might ask, 'Would you like a towel and soap with that?' One of the things you can expect from the Köbes is that even if you have not ordered, you will be served with a beer with a comment like, 'That will keep you busy and I won't have to run around after you'.

EXCURSIONS

HAFENTERRASSE (113 F5) (*ﾉﾉ G6*)
At the Malakoff Tower and the swing bridge before the Chocolate Museum. Drinks are served, but you choose your own snacks

Sushi or *Sauerbraten*? In Cologne, you can choose between cuisine from all over the world or hearty traditional fare in a *Brauhaus*

at the INSIDER TIP booth, used in the German *Tatort* series. *April–Oct daily 11am–11pm | Rheinauhafen 1 a | tel. 0221 2 72 02 62 | U 3, 4: Severinstraße | Budget*

KAHNSTATION IM BLÜCHERPARK (113 D1) (*ℳ D1*)

Ehrenfeld's green belt with beer terraces, ponds and playgrounds. Live music on weekends. *Daily 2pm–1am, Sun from 10am | http://the-pluesh.de | Parkgürtel/ Blücherpark | tel. 0221 17 02 29 1 | U 13: Nußbaumer Straße | Budget*

BEER GARDENS

INSIDER TIP AACHENER WEIHER (115 D5) (*ℳ D5*)

On warm evenings the beer garden and the surrounding meadows are a popular place for students and the in-crowd. Different summer and winter menus ranging from steak to half a duck. *Daily 11am–midnight | Richard-Wagner-Straße | tel. 0221 5 00 06 14 or 5 08 04 27 | www. biergarten-aachenerweiher.de | U 1, 7: Universitätsstraße | Budget*

A lot of Kölsch in Päffgen

INSIDER TIP RATHENAUPLATZ
(119 E1) (*∅ E6*)

Shady trees, reasonable prices and young people from the students' quarter. *Daily noon–11pm | Rathenauplatz | tel. 0221 8 01 73 49 | U-Bahn and buses: Zülpicher Platz | Budget*

STADTGARTEN (115 D–E4) (*∅ E4*)

A huge terrace area, beer and cocktails. Very busy during the weekends. Hip customers in the 20 to 40 year-old age range. *Daily noon–midnight | Venloer Straße 40 |* tel. 0211 9 52 99 42 33 | www.stadtgarten. de | U 3, 4, 5: Hans-Böckler-Platz | *Budget*

BRAUHAUS & PUBS

BIERESEL (112 C3) (*∅ F5*)

During the winter, you can choose from 24 different mussel dishes. Aside from that, homemade traditional fare is served. *Daily | Breite Straße 114 | tel. 0221 2 57 60 90 | U-Bahn and buses: Neumarkt | Budget*

FRÜH AM DOM/HOFBRÄUSTUBEN ●
(113 E2) (*∅ G4*)

One of Cologne's largest *Brauhaus* with its huge terrace and seating for 900 people in the different halls. Upstairs things are less rustic with large portions of more upscale local dishes (like guinea fowl). Try the INSIDER TIP *Deck un Dönn* or *Stippeföttche* schnapps. *Daily | Am Hof 12–14 | tel. 0221 2 61 32 11 | U/S-Bahn and buses: Dom/Hauptbahnhof | Budget*

INSIDER TIP FRÜH EM VEEDEL
(120 A2) (*∅ G7*)

A place with a true Kölsch neighbourhood atmosphere. Classic Rhine dishes are served. *Sun closed | Chlodwigplatz 28 | tel. 0221 31 44 70 | buses 132, 133, U 6, 15, 16: Chlodwigplatz | Budget*

MALZMÜHLE (113 E4) (*∅ G5*)

After a visit by the former US President they renamed their *Sauerbraten* and it is now called the 'Clinton' dish. The Köbes' tradition has been handed down, 'Two beer or not two beer?' *Daily | Heumarkt 6 | tel. 0221 21 01 17 | www.muehlenkoelsch.de | U-Bahn and buses: Heumarkt | Budget*

PÄFFGEN ● (112 B2) (*∅ E4*)

Regulars discuss world events over a Kölsch. Lovely beer garden. If you are very hungry then try the *Grillhaxe* or pork knuckle! *Daily | Friesenstraße 64–66 | tel.*

*0221 13 54 61 | www.paeffgen-koelsch.de |
U-Bahn and buses: Friesenplatz | Budget*

PETERS BRAUHAUS
⭐ (113 E3) *(ᗉ G5)*

A beautiful interior with an art nouveau stained-glass ceiling – and the Köbes are friendly. For the calorie-conscious, try the 'Tünnes und Schäl' salad. *Daily | Mühlengasse 1 | tel. 0221 2 57 39 50 | www.petersbrauhaus.de | U/S-Bahn and buses: Dom/Hauptbahnhof | Budget*

INSIDER TIP PUSZTA-HÜTTE
(112 C4) *(ᗉ F5)*

They only serve goulash – the best in the city. Second helpings of sauce are free. *Sun closed | Fleischmengergasse 57 | tel. 0221 23 94 71 | www.pusztahuette.de | U-Bahn and buses: Neumarkt | Budget*

INSIDER TIP SCHRECKENSKAMMER ●
(115 F4) *(ᗉ F4)*

Smallest and oldest brewery pub – it dates back to AD 580! The floor is strewn with sand and the waiters wear the authentic blue waistcoats. *Closed Sun | Ursulagartenstraße 11 | tel. 0221 13 25 81 | U/S-Bahn and buses: Dom/Hauptbahnhof or Hansaring | Budget*

CAFÉS

CAFÉ REICHARD ☼ (113 D2) *(ᗉ F4)*

You will have the best view of the cathedral from the terrace. The pastries are top class – but come at a price. *Daily | Unter Fettenhennen 11 | tel. 0221 2 57 85 42 | www.cafe-reichard.de | U/S-Bahn and buses: Dom/Hauptbahnhof | Budget*

HARDROCK CAFÉ (113 E4) *(ᗉ G5)*

Well-known US chain with memorabilia from Elvis Presley to Madonna. *Daily | Gürzenichstraße 8 | tel. 0221 2 72 68 80 | U-Bahn and buses: Heumarkt | Budget*

TRÖDELCAFÉ UND ANTIKES
(113 D4) *(ᗉ F5)*

A mixture between a coffee shop and junk shop, the furnishings are for sale. *Daily | An St Agatha 29 | tel. 0221 2 58 02 28 | U-Bahn and buses: Heumarkt | Budget*

LIGHT MEALS

CURRY COLOGNE
(115 D4) *(ᗉ D4)*

If you wish, you can even drink Champagne with your Berliner Currywurst. *Daily | Antwerpener Straße 5 | tel. 0221 5 89 45 56 | www.currycologne.de | U-Bahn and buses: Friesenplatz | Budget*

MOSCHMOSCH
(112 B3) *(ᗉ E4)*

Japanese snack bar. Their speciality is the steamed buns *nikuman*. The noodle soup, fried noodles and many other dishes are healthy and low in fat. *Daily | Pfeilstraße 25–27 | tel. 0221 9 65 77 67 | www.moschmosch.com | U-Bahn and buses: Rudolfplatz | Budget*

⭐ **Peters Brauhaus**
Excellent Rhineland cuisine
→ p. 57

⭐ **Le Moissonnier**
Creative and eccentric: enjoy French haute cuisine → p. 58

⭐ **Nikko**
Popular and authentic: the best Japanese in Cologne
→ p. 61

⭐ **Zur Tant**
Creative dishes and a beautiful view of the Rhine
→ p. 61

MARCO POLO HIGHLIGHTS

LIGHT MEALS

SPEISEMEISTER
(114 B2) (𝄞 C2)
A mix of good home cooking and the exotic at snack bar prices. *Sun closed | Subbelrather Straße 299 | tel. 0221 2 50 77 62 | U5: Subbelrather Straße/Gürtel | Budget*

SUSHI NARA (112 A3) (𝄞 E4)
Watch the preparation first and then eat: this little bar can only accommodate a few customers, but the selection of tea and sushi is great. Take-aways are also available. *Daily | Friesenstraße 70 | tel. 0221 12 01 70 | U-Bahn and buses: Friesenplatz | Budget*

GOURMET RESTAURANTS

Gut Lärchenhof (0) (𝄞 0)
Not just for members of the golf club. Stylish but relaxed atmosphere. The kitchen serves unusual combinations of fish and vegetables. 4-course menu 65 euros. *Daily noon–2pm and 6–10pm | Hahnenstraße | Pulheim-Stommeln | tel. 0223 8 92 31 00 | www.restaurant-gutlaerchenhof.de | RE 8 and RE 18: Stommeln, bus 876: Wiesenhof, by car: Venloer Straße to Stommeln*

Hanse-Stube Excelsior
(113 D–E2) (𝄞 G4)
The critics agree: this excellent restaurant deserves a Michelin star! Wine list with over 600 labels. 3-course menu 29 euros afternoon, 64 euros evening. *Daily noon–2.30pm and 6–11.30pm | Trankgasse 1–5/Dom | online table reservations or tel. 0221 27 01 | www.excelsior hotelernst.de | U-Bahn and buses: Dom/Hauptbahnhof*

Le Moissonnier ★
(115 F2) (𝄞 F3)
This relaxed and informal art nouveau restaurant has been one of Cologne's top addresses for years. Head chef Eric Menchon uses classic French cuisine as inspiration to create his new dishes. 4-course menu from 65 euros, main dishes 34–48 euros. *Closed Sun/Mon | Krefelder Straße 25 | tel. 0221 72 94 79 | www.lemoissonnier.de | U/S-Bahn: Hansaring*

Schlosshotel Lerbach (0) (𝄞 0)
One of the region's best restaurants is Lerbach in the Schlosshotel. It has garnered three Michelin stars and 19 Gault Millau points, its most coveted tables are the ones that overlook the romantic castle grounds. 5-course menu 135–145 euros, 7-course menu 170 euros, main dishes about 50 euros. *Closed Sun/Mon | Lerbacher Weg | Bergisch-Gladbach | tel. 0 22 02 20 40 | www.schlosshotel-lerbach.com | S 11: Bergisch Gladbach, bus 454: Lerbacher Weg; by car: A 4, exit 19, Bensberg*

La Vision in the Wasserturm
(112 C5) (𝄞 F6)
This Michelin starred restaurant with its elegant and classical style on the 11th floor of the Wasserturm Hotel, serves creative haute cuisine. Menu prices: 3-course 73 euros, 4-course 88 euros, 5-course 103 euros, 6-course 118 euros. *Closed Sun/Mon | Kaygasse 2 | tel. 0221 2 00 80 | www.hotel-im-wasserturm.de | U-Bahn and buses: Appellhofplatz*

RESTAURANTS: EXPENSIVE

CASA DI BIASE BRASSERIA
(119 E1) (*⑰ E7*)

Good value, refined Italian dishes. The chef does away with the superfluous extras that you would normally find in a gourmet restaurant. *Sat evenings only, Sun closed | Eifelplatz 4 | tel. 0221 32 24 33 | www.casadibiase.de | U12: Eifelplatz*

DAITOKAI (112 C2) (*⑰ F4*)

Sit right next to the grill and watch your food being prepared for you. The chefs give circus-like performances with their razor sharp knives. Menus between 40 and 66 euros. *Mon and Tue afternoons closed | Kattenbug 2 | tel. 0221 12 00 48 | www.daitokai.de | U-Bahn and buses: Appellhofplatz*

LE MEROU IN THE DOM HOTEL ☼
(113 D2) (*⑰ G4*)

International hotel guests and Cologne's citizens enjoy first-class cuisine in an elegant building. *Daily 6am–11pm | Domkloster 2 a | tel. 0221 2 02 40 | U/S-Bahn and buses: Dom/Hauptbahnhof*

LES TROIS B/CLUB ASTORIA (0) (*⑰ 0*)

Bistro restaurant in a former Belgian officers' club with seasonal menus and dishes with a French-Mediterranean twist. A small menu of coffee and cake is available from 3–6pm. Terrace with beautiful views of the Adenauer pond. *Mon closed | Guths-Muths-Weg 3 | tel. 0221 9 87 45 10 | www.club-astoria.eu | U1: Rheinenergiestadion*

RESTAURANTS: MODERATE

INSIDER TIP ▶ BOSPORUS
(116 A3) (*⑰ F3*)

Haute cuisine, oriental origins with Western-Mediterranean influences. Rec-

Watch first, and then eat: Kyoto

ommended: *Sultan Sac*, tender lamb strips with a garlic and yoghurt herb sauce. The terrace is very popular in the summer. *Closed Sun afternoons | Weidengasse 36 | tel. 0221 12 52 65 | www.bosporus. de | U-Bahn and buses: Breslauer Platz/ Ebertplatz*

HEISING UND ADELMANN
(112 A3) (*⑰ E4*)

Upmarket urban ambience combined with a relaxed atmosphere makes this a popular meeting place for trendy media types. Bar, large restaurant and cosy beer garden. Creative cross-cultural cooking. *Closed afternoons and Sun/Mon | Friesenstraße 58–60 | tel. 0221 130 94 24 | www. heising-und-adelmann.de | U-Bahn and buses: Friesenplatz*

LOCAL SPECIALITIES

▶ **Flönz** – *Blutwurst* (blood sausage) with large pieces of bacon

▶ **Halve Hahn** – rye bread with Dutch cheese and mustard

▶ **Himmel un Ääd** – apples (heaven) and potatoes (earth) are boiled and pureed and then served with fried *Flönz*

▶ **Kölsch** – top-fermented light beer with approx. 4.8 per cent alcohol, which may only be brewed in Cologne and served in tall glasses

▶ **Kölsche Kaviar** – *Flönz* with onions, black bread or *Röggelchen* (rye roll)

▶ **Krüstchen** – small snacks served in a small bowl. A *Krüstchen* of goulash would be a small bowl of goulash with a rye roll

▶ **Muuze and Muuzemandeln** – traditional donut-like pastries served during carnival time

▶ **Rheinischer Heringsstipp** – herrings pickled with onions, apples, gherkins and mustard seeds in a vinegar and cream sauce and served with boiled potatoes

▶ **Rheinische Muscheln** – mussles cooked with onions, carrots, leeks, bay leaves and white wine (photo right)

▶ **Rheinische Sauerbraten** – mostly made from beef, but the experts prefer horse meat! The meat marinades in vinegar, onions, juniper berries, peppercorns and vegetables for three to four days. The sauce is flavoured with raisins. Traditional accompaniment: apple sauce and potato dumplings (photo left)

▶ **Rievkooche** – potato fritters made from a batter of grated potato mixed with milk, eggs, flour and salt and fried in oil

▶ **Schavu** – Savoy cabbage

KYOTO (115 D5) (*ΩΩ D5*)

Authentic Japanese cooking and there are lunch menus for only 11 euros. You can also make your own sushi combinations. Delicious tip for tables of 3 to 4 persons: the **INSIDER TIP** Japanese fondue pot. *Closed Sun | Brüsseler Straße 12 | tel. 0221 2 40 46 64 | U-Bahn and buses: Rudolfplatz*

MAYBACH (115 E3) (*ΩΩ F3*)

This restaurant and beer garden is situated next to the cinema in the Mediapark – most of the guests are from the media industry. Original East German décor, Mediterranean cooking, good choice of wines. *Daily | Maybachstraße 111 | tel. 0221*

9 12 35 98 | www.maybach111.de | U/S-Bahn and buses: Hansaring

NIKKO ★ (118 C1) (*ØJ G5*)

Fabulous appetiser menu, excellent sushi and sashimi. Reservations essential! *Sat and Sun afternoon closed | Dürener Straße 89 | tel. 0221 4 00 00 94 | www.nikko-koeln.de | bus 136, 146: Karl-Schwering-Platz*

ZUR TANT ★ ☀ (O) (*ØJ O*)

Not to be confused with the inner city traditional restaurant *Bei d'r Tant*. The creative cooking and great views of the Rhine justifies the trip to Porz-Langel. *Thu closed | Rheinbergstraße 49 | tel. 02203 8 18 83 | www.zurtant.de | bus 164, 501: Sandbergstraße*

RESTAURANTS: BUDGET

ALCAZAR (115 D4) (*ØJ D–E4*)

Reservations are not possible: you have to arrive early and wait at the bar for a table. The traditional Austrian dish *Tafelspitz* (boiled beef) would not taste better in Vienna. For the most part Mediterranean influenced menu is served. *Sat and Sun afternoon closed | Bismarckstraße 39 a | tel. 0221 51 57 33 | U-Bahn and buses: Friesenplatz*

GOLDMUND ● (114 C3) (*ØJ C3*)

A literary café where you can select a suitable book from the shelves to enjoy with your coffee. *Daily | Glasstraße 2 | tel. 0221 5 34 15 84 | www.goldmundkoeln.de | U, 3, 4, 13: Venloer Straße/Gürtel*

SOUPPRESSO ☺ (112 B3) (*ØJ E5*)

Organic restaurant, tailored to vegetarians and vegans, as well as to guests who require gluten free food or for those with allergies. The daily and weekly menus include a variety of soups, quiches, salads, pasta dishes and cake. *Sun only by request |*

Apostelnstraße 19 | tel. 0221 99 87 89 54 | www.souppresso-bio.de | U-Bahn and buses: Neumarkt

WINE BARS

DELIX FOOD AND WINE (112 A3) (*ØJ E4*)

Dirk Middendorf brought the concept from New York: combination of a delicatessen and a coffee bar with wines from Spain, Chile, South Africa and the USA. *Closed Sun | Friesenstraße 72–74 | tel. 0221 1 26 02 00 | U-Bahn and buses: Friesenplatz*

WEINHAUS VOGEL (116 A3–4) (*ØJ G3*)

Most guests choose to drink beer, but the very traditional atmosphere of this wine bar makes it worth a visit. An unwritten law means that standing space at the bar is reserved for regulars. *Daily | from 10am | Eigelstein 74 | tel. 0221 13 99 134 | U-Bahn and buses: Ebertplatz or Breslauer Platz*

LOW BUDGET

▶ In the expensive Altstadt the *Kaffeebud om Aldermaat (Alter Markt 58–60 | U-Bahn and buses: Heumarkt* (113 E3) (*ØJ G5*)) is an oasis for the budget-conscious. Apart from coffee they also serve Bockwurst, goulash soup and snacks.

▶ For good and inexpensive coffee try the *Domforum (Mon–Fri until 6.30pm, Sat/Sun until 5pm | Domkloster 3 | tel. 0221 92 58 47 20 | www.domforum.de | U/S-Bahn and buses: Dom/Hauptbahnhof* (113 D2) (*ØJ F4*)), situated directly opposite the cathedral

SHOPPING

CITY WHERE TO START?
Neumarkt (112 B–C 3–4)
(📖 F5) is where to start your shopping spree: the Schildergasse precinct starts here. With 17,000 visitors per hour it is rated as Europe's number one shopping street. To the north is the Neumarkt-Galerie mall and the Neumarkt-Passage arcade – perfect on a rainy day. On Mittelstraße to the west you'll find everything from designer boutiques to sport shops within a radius of 500 metres.

Are you looking for a Cologne memento? T-shirts, coasters and ashtrays with the cathedral are in all likelihood produced somewhere in the Far East. So if you prefer something authentic then rather visit *Printen Schmitz*.

Here you can buy the cathedral in edible form as well as many other cute items made of marzipan that are almost too pretty to eat. The large stores can be found in *Hohe Straße* and *Schildergasse*. The pedestrian zone connects to the *Neumarkt* shopping arcade. The specialist shops for masks, costumes, décor and event material are open year round because Cologne is a party city and the party does not end

Photo: Olivandenhof

Design, delicatessens and dress-up fun: Cologne even beats London when it comes to shopping

after carnival! When a number of art galleries moved to Berlin, the art scene in Cologne dwindled and now most of the avant-garde galleries are concentrated around two buildings in Riehl *(An der Schanz 1A | U 18: Boltensternstraße* **(117 D1)** *(🔎 J1))* and around the Süd Bridge *(Schönhauser Straße 8 | U 16: Schönhauser Straße* **(120 B3)** *(🔎 H8))*. In the inner city, the majority of shops are open until 7pm or 8pm on weekdays and Saturdays until 4pm. Opening times are only mentioned if they deviate from the norm.

ACCESSORIES & BEAUTY

BEAUTY HAIR & ACCESSORIES (112 B3) *(🔎 F5)*
Cologne's only shop where a wet shave is still done with the traditional folding

razor and strop. Large selection of combs and brushes made from natural hair. *Closed Mon | Breite Straße 161–167 | U 3, 4, 16, 18: Appellhofplatz/Breite Straße*

JÜRGEN EIFLER
(112 B3) (*E4–5*)

For some elegant head wear, try the milliner Jürgen Eifler and choose a Panama or a Borsalino for the summer. *Mon–Fri 11am–6pm, Sat 11am–4pm | Friesenwall 102a | www.hut-classic.com | U-Bahn and buses: Friesenplatz*

Straße 104 | U 3, 4, 16, 18: Appellhofplatz/Breite Straße

ANTIQUES & GALLERIES

ANTIQUARIAT SIEGFRIED UNVERZAGT
(112 A3) (*E4*)

Speciality shop for bibliophiles with emphasis on the literature of the humanities and old art books – a total of 120,000 volumes. *Mon–Fri 3–7pm, Sat 11am–3pm | Limburger Straße 10 | U-Bahn and buses: Friesenplatz*

Beautiful to wear: collection in Gesine Moritz's boutique

ROECKL (113 D3) (*F4*)
Even the Bavarian King Ludwig II was a fan of this establishment. For the last 180 years they have been producing sought after gloves made from leather, silk and lace. *Hohe Straße 160–168 | www.roeckl.com | U/S-Bahn and buses: Dom/Hauptbahnhof*

SCHIRM BURSCH (112 C3) (*F5*)
A specialist shop with umbrellas and walking sticks in all shapes and sizes that also offer custom designs. *Mon–Fri 10am–6.30pm, Sat 10am–3pm | Breite*

INSIDER TIP GALERIE THOMAS ZANDER
(120 C3) (*H8*)

Pop Art, photographic art and avant-garde by artists like Max Regenberg. *Tue–Fri 11am–6pm, Sat noon–6pm | Schönhauser Straße 8 | U 16: Schönhauser Straße*

BOUTIQUES & DESIGNER CLOTHING

GESINE MORITZ (112 C3) (*F5*)
Sophisticated and upmarket clothing collection. Elegant velvets or casual comfort

with lots of loose flowing fabrics. *Neumarkt 18 a | U-Bahn and buses: Rudolfplatz*

JOHANNA LUTZ (115 F3) (*ₒ F3*)

All the garments by designer Johanna Lutz are exquisitely individual and hand sewn. Customers appreciate her perfect patterns and extraordinary colour combinations. *Tue–Sat noon–7pm Gereonwall 13 | U/S-Bahn: Hansaring*

LABUDE (115 D6) (*ₒ D5*)

Along with her own collection of handcrafted clothing, Julia Kirstein also sells items by other young designers. Her own label Labude combines clever new ideas with fashion influences from the 1920s to the 1970s. *Tue–Fri noon–7pm, Sat noon–6pm | Lindenstraße 93 | www.labude-koeln.de | U-Bahn and buses: Rudolfplatz, U 1, 7: Moltkestraße*

MADAMSKI (112 A5) (*ₒ E6*)

Browse through the designs of new and emerging fashion labels in a comfortable and relaxed atmosphere. *Engelbertstraße 23 | entrance to the courtyard | www.madamski.de | U 9, 12, 15: Zülpicher Platz*

MARION MUCK MODE (112 B3) (*ₒ E5*)

A designer that is popular with German celebrities, also stocks shoes and accessories. *Kleine Brinkgasse 41 a | U-Bahn and buses: Rudolfplatz*

TAUSEND FLIEGENDE FISCHE (112 A5) (*ₒ E6*)

This colourful boutique offers a large collection of both well known and new labels. *Roonstraße 16 | U-Bahn and buses: Zülpicher Platz*

VELANGEL ⏱ (112 A4) (*ₒ E5*)

Barbara Lehmann's fashion designs are carefree and casual, yet appealing and sophisticated. Many pieces are made out with organic fabrics. *Tue–Fri 11am–7pm, Sat noon–6pm | Engelbertstraße 51 | www.velangel.de | U-Bahn and buses: Zülpicher Platz*

DELICATESSENS

INSIDER TIP ▶ BÄRENDRECK-APOTHEKE ⏱ (112 A4) (*ₒ E5*)

At this 'pharmacy' you will not find any pills just 350 different sorts of liquorice sweets from all over the world, even gluten or sugar free. *Tue–Fri noon–6.30pm, Sat noon–4.30pm | Richard-Wagner-Straße 1 | www.baerendreck-apotheke.de | U-Bahn and buses: Rudolfplatz*

HONIG-MÜNGERSDORFF (113 D4) (*ₒ F5*)

This family business has been involved with honey since 1847. Not only do they sell jars of honey but also sweets, liqueurs and wines all made from honey. *An St Agatha 37 | U-Bahn and buses: Neumarkt*

★ Hoss an der Oper
A gourmet's delight – culinary treasures and delicacies from all over the world → p. 66

★ Balloni
Ideal for party hosts and decorators in search of something original → p. 67

★ Filz Gnoss
No more cold feet – just one of the many properties of felt → p. 69

★ Nippes
Indigenous and exotic fruit at the weekly market → p. 69

MARCO POLO HIGHLIGHTS

HOSS AN DER OPER ★
(113 D3) (*ⅉ F5*)

A gourmet deli that offers mouth-watering fare: fine sausages, home-made pies, desserts, salads, tinned soups and even 90-year old Armagnac. *Closed Mon | Breite Straße 25–27 | U-Bahn and buses: Appellhofplatz*

INSIDER TIP ▶ PRINTEN SCHMITZ
(112 C3) (*ⅉ F5*)

Delicious cakes and pastries, pralines and marzipan creations – since 1842! *Breite Straße 87 | U-Bahn and buses: Appellhofplatz*

WILD-GEFLÜGEL BROCK
(112 B3) (*ⅉ E5*)

A traditional butcher shop with an original interior dating back to 1930. Some culinary delicacies like quail eggs and pies and a wide selection of treats sold in jars and tins. *Aposteinstraße 44 | U-Bahn and buses: Neumarkt*

LOW BUDGET

▶ It need not always be the latest tennis racquet or jogging outfit or some expensive top brand, instead you can find sports clothing at discounted prices at *Muskelkater. Aachener Straße 76 | www.muskel katersport.de | U-Bahn and buses: Rudolfplatz* **(115 D5)** (*ⅉ D5*)

▶ Bric-a-brac, porcelain, old books, furniture and rarities: you will find the kinds of beautiful pieces that could become heirlooms at the *Flohmarkthalle Köln (Mauritiussteinweg 100 | www.flohmarkthalle-koeln. de | U-Bahn and buses: Neumarkt* **(114 B4)** (*ⅉ E5*))

ZWÖLF GRAD
(119 F2) (*ⅉ F7*)

Witty shop fittings: all the shelves are tilted at 12 degrees. Wines from small wine farms in Germany and France. *Martin-Luther-Platz 1 | U-Bahn and buses: Chlodwigplatz*

DESIGN

GEMISCHTWAREN.COM
(114 C3) (*ⅉ D3*)

Thor Zimmermann's shop has quirky items like adhesive plaster with Swarovski crystals by designer Fabian Seibert or an instant ice-maker. There are also some useful items alongside the fun stuff. You will see things that you do not need, but also cannot live without! *Thu/Fri 11am–7pm, Sat noon–4pm | Körner Straße 68 | www.gemischtwaren.com | U 3, 4: Körner Straße*

GESCHMACKSSACHEN (114 C3) (*ⅉ C3*)

Bizarre lights, whimsical décor, retro key holders and objets d'art at reasonable prices: one of the most original designer shops in Cologne – well worth a browse. *Tue–Thu 2–6pm, Fri 11am–1.30pm and 5–7pm, Sat 11am–4pm | Körner Straße 56 | www.geschmackssachen.com | U 3, 4: Körner Straße*

KO-J ☺ (118 C3) (*ⅉ D7*)

In the Sülz district, Sybille Hansen sells cushions, lamps, tables, cups and many other items. Everything is made from recycled materials and is produced in Indonesia through fair trade practices. *Tue–Fri 10am–1pm and 2.30–6.30pm, Sat 10am–3pm | Berrenrather Straße 205 | www.ko-j.de | U 18: Sülzburgstraße*

PETER GÜLS (112 C3) (*ⅉ F5*)

Jewellery designer Peter Güls designs extravagant necklaces and rings from matt black iron that is combined with fiery red coral or glittering pearls. The bracelets, pendants and chains look striking and unusual. *Mon–Fri 10am–6pm, Sat 10am–2pm | Breite Straße 97 | U 3, 16, 18: Appellhofplatz/Breite Straße*

INSIDER TIP ▶ **FESTARTIKEL SCHMITT** (116 B3) (ⵁ G4)
Just seeing all their Indian, gypsy, sailor or pirate costumes, will put you in the mood to dress up. There are three floors filled with confetti, glitter, stage make-up, cos-

A whole range of offbeat things: a matter of taste

CARNIVAL & PARTY SUPPLIES

BALLONI ★ (114 C3) (ⵁ C3)
Unusual party supplies and quirky table decorations: tablecloths, decorative fabrics, balloons, confetti, glitter, stars and much more. *Ehrenfeldgürtel 88–94 | U 3, 4, 13: Venloer Straße/Gürtel*

DEITERS (113 E4) (ⵁ G5)
Whether it is for the Rose Monday parade or any other party, here you will find all sorts of fancy dress costumes and hats. *Gürzenichstraße 25 | U-Bahn and buses: Heumarkt*

tume jewellery, garlands and sparklers, where you can shop all-year round. *Mon–Fri 10am–7pm, Sat 11am–3pm | Johannisstraße 67 | U-Bahn: Breslauer Platz*

DER KARNEVALSWIERTS (0) (ⵁ 0)
Would you like to dress up as a clown, a fluffy bunny or a nun dressed in pink – but not just to the carnival? Then you should travel to Godorf in southern Cologne. In this 6500 ft² hall you can choose from over 400 different costumes during the whole year (approx. 40 to 50 euros) and your next fancy dress party outfit will be in the bag. *Otto-Hahn-Straße 17 | bus 135: Otto-Hahn-Straße, U 16: Godorf*

MUSIC

MUSIC

MUSIKHAUS TONGER
(113 D3) (*M F5*)
Everything for professional and amateur musicians: tuning forks, music stands, music scores, instruments and more. *Breite Straße 2 | www.musik-tonger.de | U 3, 4, 16, 18: Appellhofplatz/Breite Straße*

SCHALLHANDEL (119 E1) (*M E6*)
This **INSIDER TIP** vinyl record specialist also stocks a selection of CDs and DVDs. From rock 'n'roll and psychobilly to hip hop and jazz all the genres from the past 60 years are represented. *Luxemburger Straße 72 | U 18: Eifelwall*

PEDESTRIAN ARCADES

DUMONT-CARRÉ (112 C3) (*M F5*)
Browse the photo exhibitions in *Studio Dumont* and then try out one of the city's best ice-cream stands. The blueberry muffins at *Henry's Coffeeworld* are also top class. *Breite Straße 80–90 | U-Bahn and buses: Appellhofplatz/Breite Straße*

NEUMARKT-GALERIE
(112 C3) (*M F5*)
When you see the large ice-cream cone by Claes Oldenburg on its roof, you know you are on the right track. There are 67 shops to choose from for all your needs and special wishes. Integrated in the building complex, is the *Richmodisturm*, two horse sculptures looking out of the window. This is based on a Cologne legend: during the 14th century Mrs Richmodis von Aducht's husband did not believe that his wife was really dead, saying that he would only believe it if his horses left the stable and came into his room. A while later, hooves could be heard coming up the stairs ... *Richmodstraße 8 | U-Bahn and buses: Neumarkt*

NEUMARKT-PASSAGE ●
(114 B-C3) (*M F5*)
Besides shops, boutiques and cafés, you will also find the Käthe Kollwitz Museum and the Lew Kopelew Forum here. *Neumarkt | www.neumarktpassage. de | U-Bahn and buses: Neumarkt*

OLIVANDENHOF (112 C3) (*M F5*)
The outdoor specialist shop Globetrotter stretches over four floors with different departments. A large water sports pool in the basement allows you to test boating or diving equipment.

OPERNPASSAGEN
(112 C–D3) (*M F5*)
Apart from gift shops, fashion and a piano shop, you will also find cafés and restaurants – ideal for a snack after the opera or the Theater am Dom. *Corner of Breite Straße/Neue Langgasse | U-Bahn and buses: Appellhofplatz*

SHOES

BIOLINE ☺
(113 D3) (*M F5*)
This company's philosophy: only natural materials and nothing chunky or staid. *Minoritenstraße 1 | U/S-Bahn and buses: Dom/Hauptbahnhof*

FOLLOW ME (112 A5) (*M E6*)
Trendy shoe brands like Bronx and Vagabond, but they also stock other brands. If you prefer your outfits to be cutting-edge, this is where to buy your shoes. *Zülpicher Platz 12 | U-Bahn and buses: Zülpicher Platz*

ZU FUSS (112 B3) (*M E5*)
Embroidered leather slip-ons (approx. 75 euros), elegant ladies' boots, sporty and robust shoes. *Ehrenstraße 96–98 | U-Bahn and buses: Friesenplatz*

SECOND-HAND

ENTLARVT (112 B3) (*Ⓜ E6*)
This second-hand shop in the university quarter specialises in fashion from the 1960s and 1970s. They also sell a range of used stage costumes. *Zülpicher Straße 6 | U-Bahn and buses: Zülpicher Platz*

DIE GARDEROBE (114 C3) (*Ⓜ C3*)
The stock is made up of hippy fashion from the 1960s (with lots of bright colours) through to chic modern fashions. Special feature: everything is arranged according to colour. *Körnerstraße 29 | U 3, 4: Körnerstraße*

FABRIC

FILZ GNOSS ★
(112 B3) (*Ⓜ E5*)
Everything sold here is made from felt: slippers, hats, furniture padding, sound proofing – all made from this traditional material. Also: hobby and technical felt.

Apostelnstraße 21 | U-Bahn and buses: Neumarkt

WEEKLY MARKETS

In Cologne there are about 39 regular weekly markets but two of the markets deserve special mention for their atmosphere and the range on offer:

APOSTELNKLOSTER (112 B3–4) (*Ⓜ E5*)
Wonderful flower stands, herbs and oils, fruits and vegetables: a little bit of Provence under the shady trees. *Tue and Fri 7am–1pm | Apostelnkloster | U-Bahn and buses: Neumarkt*

NIPPES ★ (116 A1) (*Ⓜ F1*)
A farmers market with lots of food and fresh vegetables where all the stall holders speak Kölsch so: *Kätteschloot* for dandelions, *Öllich* for onions and *Sprütcher* for Brussel sprouts. *Mon–Fri 7am–1pm, Sat 7am–2.30pm | Wilhelmplatz | U 6, 12, 18: Florastraße*

A special treat for many: shopping at the weekly market

ENTERTAINMENT

CITY **WHERE TO START?**
Start your night on **Friesen-platz (112 A2)** *(🚇 E4)*. From here you are only a few steps from the popular Belgian Quarter and only 10–12 minutes by foot (or two stations to Zülpicher Platz) to the student pubs in the *Kwartier lateng* or Latin Quarter between Rathenau-platz and Luxemburger Straße. Chic and trendy cocktail, tapas and sushi bars line Friesenstraße while the dance clubs can be found in the area around Friesenplatz.

Drink doch ene met, stell dich nit esu an **(Drink another one with us, don't be so stuck up), is one of the songs of the band Bläck Föös. Rhinelanders are social and love to swap their living room for the pub.** Cologne's gastronomy is not only limited to its Kölsch pubs, it also offers a club culture that ranges from jazzy cocktail bars to places playing Latin, salsa, drum-and-base, soul or funk and there are a couple of nightlife areas in the city centre. The *Martinsviertel* (Altstadt) offers some fast paced fun. Current events are advertised with flyers and posters. The pubs between Waidmarkt and Heumarkt are popular with Cologne's gay community.

Photo: Nachtflug nightclub

Paint the town red: the theatres, the clubs and the cocktail bars will keep you busy as there is so much more to Cologne than the carnival!

DANCING & CLUBS

ALTER WARTESAAL (113 E2) (*ω G4*)
Every month for the past 20 years they have held a monthly Depeche Mode Party here. Other regular events in this old train waiting room include the Hootchie Cootchie Club evenings which cater to the musical tastes of those past their teenage years. *Restaurant kitchen open until 11.30pm, Sun brunch from 10.30am, club Fri/Sat depending on event | Johanisstraße 11 (Hauptbahnhof) | www.wartesaal.de | U/S-Bahn and buses: Dom/Hauptbahnhof*

ARTHEATER (114 C3) (*ω C2–3*)
Mainly viewed as a techno temple with house and electronic parties. *Sat 10pm– 5am, otherwise according to event | Ehrenfeldgürtel 127 | tel. 0221 5 50 33 44 | night*

Jazz in Studio 672 which is part of the complex at Stadtgarten

cashier: tel. 0221 5 50 99 60 | buses 141, 142: Ehrenfeldgürtel, U 3, 4: Venloer Straße/Ehrenfeldgürtel

GEBÄUDE 9 (117 D3) (⚹ J3)
Just behind the exhibition centre and Zoo Bridge is an old rubber band factory that is a venue for concerts and parties. The studio next door offers whacky art exhibitions. *Open according to event | Deutz-Mülheimer Straße 127–129 | tel. 0221 81 46 37 | www.gebauede9.de | U 3, 4: Koelnmesse*

LIVE MUSIC HALL (114 B3) (⚹ B3)
Live indie and electronic concerts and regular dance parties with musical themes. *Fri from 9pm, Sat from 10pm | Lichtstraße 30 | tel. 0221 9 54 29 90 | buses 141, 142: Ehrenfeldgürtel | U 3, 4: Venloer Straße/Ehrenfeldgürtel*

NACHTFLUG (112 A2) (⚹ E4)
Large club at the Hohenzollernring, where things only get going after midnight. For lovers of house music, dancefloor, soul, black music, Latin and R 'n' B. *Tue, Fri/Sat from 10pm | Hohenzollernring 89–93 | tel. 0221 5 10 22 29 | www.nachtflug.com | U-Bahn and buses: Friesenplatz*

INSIDER TIP ODONIEN (115 E2) (⚹ E2)
Between the old abattoir and two brothels, the sculptor Odo Rumpf uses a scrap yard as an open air studio, which he has declared to be 'the free state of Odonien'. The aim being that artists and performers can work here and be self-sufficient. During the warmer seasons, off-beat parties, concerts and performances take place here. *Open according to event | Horn-*

straße 85 | www.odonien.org | U 5: Gutenbergstraße

ROSE CLUB (119 E1) (*Ø E6*)

An indie-pop club with a programme for 20 to 25 year-olds. The drinks are relatively affordable compared to other clubs. The club offers a different party line-up every evening. *Tue from 10pm, Mon–Sat from 11pm | Luxemburger Straße 37 | tel. 0221 2 40 82 66 | www.rose-club-cologne. de | U-Bahn and buses: Barbarossaplatz*

TSUNAMI CLUB (120 B2) (*Ø G7*)

If you prefer small cellar clubs, then this indie club is perfect for you. Live concerts, lectures or movie evenings alternate and it is also the venue for an award-winning poetry slam competition. *Open according to event | Im Ferkulum 9 | www.tsunami-club.de | U-Bahn and buses: Chlodwigplatz*

UNDERGROUND (116 B3) (*Ø C3*)

The large bar area is complemented by two stages and a lovely beer garden. Even though the graffiti interior is somewhat dated, the music is very cutting-edge. *Daily from 6.30pm | Vogelsanger Straße 200 | tel. 0221 54 23 26 | www.underground-cologne.de | U 3, 4: Venloer Straße/ Ehrenfeldgürtel*

JAZZ

LOFT (114 C3) (*Ø D3*)

Jazz and contemporary music. *Opening times vary | Wißmannstraße 30 | tel. 0221 9 52 15 55 | www.loftkoeln.de | U 5: Liebigstraße*

MELODY PIANO BAR (118 C1) (*Ø C6*)

Wholesome location for an elegant middle-class aged between 35 and 50. Often spontaneous live sessions. *Sun–Thu 7.30pm–2am, Fri/Sat 7.30pm–3am | Dürener Straße 169 | tel. 0221 40 82 36 | bus 136: Karl-Schwering-Platz, U 2, 13: Dürener Straße/Lindenthalgürtel*

STADTGARTEN (115 D4) (*Ø E4*)

Jazz festivals, pop and rock concerts, lectures and discussion groups. *Open according to event | Venloer Straße 40 | tel. 0221 95 29 94 21 | www.stadtgarten.de | U-Bahn and buses: Hans-Böckler-Platz*

CLASSICAL

INSIDER TIP ▶ **C. BECHSTEIN CENTRUM** ● (112 C3) (*Ø F5*)

The classics in a relaxed atmosphere: free concerts by exam candidates from the music college. *Thu 5pm | Opernpassagen,*

★ **Kölner Philharmonie**
Acoustics, music, architecture – it all impresses! → p. 74

★ **1460 — Galerie & Lounge**
Sip your drink in style in its vaulted cellar → p. 74

★ **Rosebud**
Cocktail bar with baroque elegance and worldly flair → p. 76

★ **Atelier-Theater**
Pass the time with witty cabaret and hot comedy → p. 77

★ **Puppenspiele der Stadt Köln**
Nowhere in Germany will you find a theatre quite like this: puppets are the stars of the stage and everything is presented in the finest Kölsch → p. 77

MARCO POLO HIGHLIGHTS

Colourful pub with a lot of character: the Alcazar

Glockengasse 6 | tel. 0221 9 25 85 00 | www.bechstein-centren.de | U 3, 4, 16, 18: Appellhofplatz/Breite Straße

KÖLNER PHILHARMONIE ★
(113 E2) *(ⓜ G4)*
Host to many international classical stars, concerts by the Gürzenich Orchestra and the Cologne Radio Symphony Orchestra, chamber music and recital evenings. *Ticket pre-sales: tel. 0221 28 02 80 | www.koelner-philharmonie.de | U/S-Bahn and buses: Dom/Hauptbahnhof*

LITERATURHAUS KÖLN (115 E3) *(ⓜ F3)*
Lectures, recitations and reference library. *Schönhauser Straße 8 | tel. 0221 9 95 55 80 | www.literaturhaus-koeln.de | U 16: Schönhauser Straße*

MUSIKHOCHSCHULE KÖLN
(116 B3) *(ⓜ F3)*
Concerts and musical theatre. Almost always free. Programme in foyer. *Unter Krahnenbäumen 87 | tel. 0221 9 12 81 80 | www.mhs-koeln.de | U-Bahn: Breslauer Platz*

MUSICALS

MUSICAL DOME (113 E1–2) *(ⓜ G4)*
The blue tent next to the bridge is impossible to miss. *Breslauer Platz/Goldgasse 1 | tel. (*) 01805 15 25 30 | www.musical-dome-koeln.de; www.kartenkaufen.de | U-Bahn: Dom/Hauptbahnhof*

LOCAL HOT SPOTS

1460 – GALERIE & LOUNGE ★
(113 E4) *(ⓜ G5)*
This vaulted cellar with its stylish bar was once part of the chapel of Klein St Martin. Today more secular things happen at the bar. *Fri/Sat from 9pm | Augustiner Straße 23–25 | www.14hundert60.de | U-Bahn and buses: Heumarkt*

ALCAZAR (115 D4) *(ⓜ D–E4)*
Clientele ranges in age from 30 to 50 years. Old anti-establishment students from the 60s and younger media artists. *Mon–Thu noon–2am, Fri until 3am, Sat 6pm–3am, Sun 5pm–1am | Bismarckstraße*

39 | tel. 0221 51 57 33 | U-Bahn and buses: Friesenplatz

ARKADIA BAR (112 B2) *(⌂ E4)*
Once a red-light district pub, this is now a place where students drink Kölsch and dance to soul and funk. *Sun–Thu 8pm–2am, Fri/Sat until 4am | Friesenstraße 52 | tel. 0221 139 26 50 | U-Bahn and buses: Friesenplatz*

BACKES (120 B2) *(⌂ G7)*
A favourite haunt for comedians from the *Stunksitzung*, crime authors and legends of the alternative scene. *Daily from 8pm | Darmstädter Straße 6 | tel. 0221 31 11 67 | U-Bahn and buses: Chlodwigplatz*

ELEKTRA (115 F3) *(⌂ F3)*
Reminiscent of a time when everyone wore white turtleneck sweaters and black horn-rimmed glasses – mixed clientele, also locals from the area, hip and cosmopolitan serving a variety of beers from all over Germany. *Daily from 7pm | Gereonswall 12–14 | U/S-Bahn and buses: Hansaring or Ebertplatz*

KING GEORGE (116 A3) *(⌂ F–G3)*
A club-cum-bar with a retro 1970s feel. With DJs, concerts and also the occasional readings. *Thu from 9pm, Fri/Sat from 10pm | Sudermanstraße 2 | U-Bahn and buses: Ebertplatz*

KLEIN KÖLN (112 B2) *(⌂ E4)*
This was once the haunt of boxers and their rather shady fans and hangers-on and even though its wild years are now over, the Kölsch milieu still lingers. *Closed Sun, Mon–Sat until 4.30am | Friesenstraße 53 | tel. 0221 25 36 76 | www.klein-koeln.com | U-Bahn and buses: Friesenplatz*

KUNSTBAR (113 E2) *(⌂ G4)*
At the main train station you will find one of the most unusual bars in Cologne: once a year a different artist is given the opportunity to redesign the interior. *Daily from 7.30pm | Chargesheimer Platz 1 | U/S-Bahn and buses: Dom/Hauptbahnhof*

LOW BUDGET (115 D5) *(⌂ D5)*
Nothing but low lighting, tequila from the barrel, beer and music yet it remains very

SPECTATOR SPORTS

The Rheinenergiestadion Müngersdorf is home to the soccer team *1. FC Köln (Sportpark Müngersdorf | Aachener Straße 999 | www.stadion-koeln.de | U 1: Stadion, S-Bahnen: Köln-Weiden West)*. The *Cologne Falcons* use the Südstadion *(Am Vorgebirgstor | www.cologne falcons.com | U 12: Pohligstraße)* as home to their German Football League. Cycle races take place at the Albert-Richter-Radbahn. The handball team *VfL Gummersbach* plays in the Lanxess Arena Deutz *(Willy-Brandt-Platz 3 | tel.*

tickets: 0221 80 20 | tel. 0221 2 80 | buses 150, 151, 153, 170, 250, 260, U 1, 3, 4, 9: Bahnhof Deutz/Lanxess Arena), as well as the ice-hockey stars of *Kölner Haie (www.haie.de)*. Fans of the *Cologne Cardinals (www.cologne cardinals.de)* flock to the baseball stadium at Sportpark Müngersdorf and from March to November it is horse racing season at the racecourse in Weidenpesch *(Rennbahnstraße 152 | tel. 0221 9 74 50 50 | www.koeln-galopp.de | U 12, 15: Scheibenstraße)*.

their rather steep prices. *Mon–Thu 9.30pm–2am, Fri, Sat 9pm–3am, Sun 9pm–2am | Heinsbergstraße 20 | tel. 0221 2 40 14 55 | U-Bahn and buses: Zülpicher Platz*

RUBINROT (114 C3) (*ⓤ C3*)

With its red-lit interior this pub preserves its rather staid past as a traditional pub. Not as chic as some of the city's cocktail bars, but good drinks and a young clientele. *Tue–Sun from 8pm, Sömmeringstraße 9 | tel. 0221 9 90 16 98 | U 3, 4: Venloer Straße/Gürtel*

SIX PACK (115 D5) (*ⓤ D5*)

Unadorned, somewhat shabby furnishings, good music, good beer, wide selection. Weekends fairly full. *Mon–Fri 8pm–3am, Sat/Sun until 5am | Aachener Straße 33 | tel. 0221 25 45 87 | U-Bahn and buses: Rudolfplatz*

INSIDER TIP ▶ WEISSER HOLUNDER (115 E4) (*ⓤ E4*)

Pub owner Karl Schiesberg once preached in the church while the priest manned the bar. The original 1950s interior makes it worth a visit. *Daily | Gladbacher Straße 48 | tel. 0221 51 34 75 | www.weisser-holunder.de | U-Bahn and buses: Christophstraße/Mediapark*

Time travel to the 1950s: in the Weißer Holunder

popular especially during weekends. *Mon–Thu 8pm–2am, Fri/Sat 4am, closed Sun | Aachener Straße 47 | www.lowbud.de | U 1: Moltkestraße*

ROONBURG (112 A5) (*ⓤ E6*)

Music club catering to students. Officially regarded as a smoking club. *Tue from 9pm, Thu–Sat from 10pm | Roonstraße 33 | tel. 0221 2 49 37 19 | www.roonburg.de | U-Bahn and buses: Zülpicher Platz*

ROSEBUD ★ (112 A6) (*ⓤ E6*)

Cologne's most elegant cocktail bar. Excellent interior and mixes – reflected in

ZOO – DIE SCHÄNKE (114 C3) (*ⓤ B2*)

The Ehrenfeld beer Helios-Kölsch and cocktails are served here. You can tell from the art on the walls that hosts, Aline and Basti like the work of street artists. During weekends a DJ supplies appropriate background music. *Daily from 8pm | Venloer Straße 434 | U 3, 4: Leyendecker Straße*

THEATRE & CABARET

According to statistics, Cologne has 60 theatres – Berlin is the only other German city which has more.

ARKADAŞ-THEATER (114 C2) (*🛈 G2*)
Cultural stage with children's and inter-cultural theatre, cinema, dancing, cabaret and festivals. *Platenstraße 32 | tel. 0221 9 55 95 10 | www.arkadastheater.de | U 5, 13: Subbelrather Straße/Gürtel*

ATELIER-THEATER ⭐
(115 D5–6) (*🛈 E5*)
The German TV comedian Tom Gerhardt started his career here: entertainment by cabaret artists. *Roonstraße 78 | tel. 0221 24 24 85 | www.ateliertheater.de | U-Bahn and buses: Zülpicher Platz*

COMEDIA COLONIA (120 A2) (*🛈 F7*)
Contemporary theatre, cabaret and comedy guest performances as well as theatre, dancing and concerts for all age groups. *Vondelstraße 4–8 | tel. 0221 88 87 70 | www.comedia-koeln.de | U 15, 16: Chlodwigplatz*

KABARETT-THEATER KLÜNGELPÜTZ
(112 B3) (*🛈 E–F5*)
Cabarets and readings. *Gertrudenstraße 24 | tickets tel. 01 52 04 44 33 68 or info@ kluengelpuetz.de | U-Bahn and buses: Neumarkt*

PUPPENSPIELE DER STADT KÖLN ⭐ ●
(113 E3) (*🛈 G5*)
In the Hänneschen Theatre, Germany's only puppets show where plays for children and adults are presented in Kölsch. *Cashier Wed–Sun 3–6pm | Eisenmarkt 2–4 | tel. 0221 2 58 12 01 | www.haenne schen.de | U-Bahn and buses: Heumarkt*

SENFTÖPFCHEN (113 E3) (*🛈 G4–5*)
First class shows and solo recitals. The cabaret stage is financed by the drink sales – so the wines are not exactly cheap. *Große Neugasse 2–4 | tel. 0221 2 58 10 58 | U/S-Bahn and buses: Dom/ Hauptbahnhof*

THEATER IM BAUTURM E.V.
(114 D–E5) (*🛈 E5*)
Sophisticated theatre with contemporary pieces. *Aachener Straße 24 | tel. 0221 52 42 42 | U-Bahn and buses: Rudolfplatz*

VOLKSTHEATER MILLOWITSCH ●
(115 E5) (*🛈 E5*)
Peter Millowitsch produces his own contemporary farces in standard German mixed with Kölsch dialect. As rival to the Hänneschen Theatre, the founder Franz Andreas Millowitsch had to move to Deutz. From the beginning of the 20th century, the puppets were replaced by real actors. *Aachener Straße 5 | tel. 0221 25 17 47 | www.millowitsch.de | U-Bahn and buses: Rudolfplatz*

LOW BUDGET

▶ If you prefer punk rock and only want to spend 6–7 euros on a ticket, you should visit the *Sonic Ballroom*. *Sun–Thu until 2am, Fri/Sat until 5am | Oscar-Jäger Straße 190 | tel. 0221 5 46 44 45 | www.sonic-ballroom.de | U 3, 4: Leyendeckerstraße* (114 B3) (*🛈 B3*)

▶ A glass of Kölsch is almost a third cheaper at *Trash Chic* than in the old town. *Daily | Wiersbergstraße 31 | tel. 0221 4 92 88 55 | www.trash-chic.com | U 1, 9: Kalk Kapelle* (117 F5) (*🛈 L5*)

▶ The *Green Bar* is not exclusively for the guests of the backpackers' hostel next door *(Sun–Thu until 1am, Fri/Sat until 3am | Rheingasse 34–36 | tel. 0221 23 02 47 | U-Bahn and buses: Heumarkt* (113 E4) (*🛈 G5*)) and is also a good choice for a cheap pint of beer.

WHERE TO STAY

Cologne boasts more than 250 hotels with 26,000 beds. However, with more than 40 trade fairs and other major events held annually, accommodation is often fully booked.

On Rose Monday, more than 1 million people turn out to watch the parade and Cologne's high society hires their own *Finster för d'r Zoch* (window for the parade) in the Excelsior Hotel Ernst. During the peak seasons, most hotels in the city increase their rates by up to 100 per cent. But on normal days even small guesthouses charge astronomical rates. Rule of thumb: the closer the hotel is to the cathedral, the more expensive the rate.

It is still possible to find affordable hotels and guesthouses in the city centre. You just have to be a fan of old wallpaper and basic furnishings. Travel agents sometimes offer affordable weekend packages. Found a hotel in the Altstadt? Then you should know that this pub-friendly neighbourhood will not be shutting up shop at 9pm: if you prefer a bit of peace and quiet, you should rather look for accommodation in the outer suburbs. Somewhere like *Sürther Falderhof* or in the Lövenicher *Gut Keuchhof*.

The local tourist service *Köln Tourismus* will arrange hotel rooms for you at a booking fee of 3 euros per booking

Photo: Hopper Hotel et cetera

The golden rule when looking for a hotel: book well in advance and you will be rewarded with the best selection

(Kardinal-Höffner-Platz 1 | tel. 0221 22 13 04 00) for same-day reservations. Early and online bookings are free. Tip: make reservations two to three weeks in advance, especially for trade fairs. Online booking: *www.koelntourismus.de*. The tourism office can also arrange private rooms.

If you want to look for affordable rooms on your own there are a number of basi-cally furnished hotels and guesthouses in the area north of the main train station and Breslauer Platz in the Domstraße/ Machabäerstraße/Johannisstraße Quarter. Some can be found in side streets like Brandenburger Straße and Jakorden-straße. But a word of caution: three blocks further in Eintrachtstraße and your 'guesthouses' could turn out to be a brothel.

ANTIK-HOTEL BRISTOL ⭐
(112 B1) (ⅉ E4)

The exceptional comes at a price but why not spend the night in a hand carved antique bed or in a gilded four-poster bed. *42 rooms| Kaiser-Wilhelm-Ring 48 | tel. 0221 12 0195 | www.antik-hotel-bristol.de | U-Bahn and buses: Christophstraße/Mediapark*

Recommended: have a drink in the Ice Bar. *296 rooms| Marzellenstraße 13–17 | tel. 0221 13 0710 | www.hilton.de | U/S-Bahn and buses: Dom/Hauptbahnhof*

HOPPER HOTEL ST ANTONIUS
(116 B3) (ⅉ G3)

The house was built in 1905 as a journeymen's hostel and was later converted to a four star hotel: historic building, modern

Sleep easy in a four-poster bed: Antik-Hotel Bristol

CRISTALL HOTEL (113 D1) (ⅉ F4)

In the breakfast room you will find lots of marble and contrasting colours. The rooms are all individually decorated and filled with original but tasteful fittings. *97 rooms | Ursulaplatz 9–11 | tel. 0221 163 00 | www. hotelcristall.de | U/S-Bahn and buses: Breslauer Platz or Dom/Hauptbahnhof*

INSIDER TIP HILTON COLOGNE HOTEL
(113 D2) (ⅉ F4)

This five star designer hotel is also a listed monument and is situated very centrally: just a two minute walk to the cathedral.

photo art on the walls and the comfort of discreet individualist interiors. PC and internet available. *39 rooms, 15 suites | Dagobertstraße 32 | tel. 0221 66 00 | www. hopper.de | U-Bahn and buses: Ebertplatz*

INTERCONTINENTAL KÖLN
(113 E4) (ⅉ G5)

Centrally located, short walking distance from the Altstadt and the shopping streets. Underground parking available at hotel. Complete business centre with internet access and the wellness rooms of the *Holmes Club (daily fee for hotel guests*

15.20 euros). 250 rooms, 12 suites | Pipinstraße 1 | tel. 0221 2 80 60 | www. koeln.intercontinental.com | U 1, 7, 9: Heumarkt

LINDNER HOTEL DOM RESIDENCE
(113 D2) (*ØJ F4*)

'Lebens Art zwischen Dom und Messe' (the art of living between the cathedral and the exhibition centre) reads the slogan on its blue glass brick facade. Straight-forward, friendly atmosphere, attentive service. 125 rooms | An den Dominikanern 4 a | entrance Stolkgasse | tel. 0221 164 40 | www.lindner.de | U/S-Bahn and buses: Dom/Hauptbahnhof

MARITIM (113 E4) (*ØJ G5*)

Large glass covered hotel foyer with a variety of shops and restaurants. Perfect conference facilities, swimming pool and fitness centre. 426 rooms, 28 suites | Heumarkt 20 | tel. 0221 2 02 70 | www. maritim.de | U-Bahn and buses: Heumarkt

INSIDER TIP ▶ THE NEW YORKER HOTEL
(117 D2–3) (*ØJ K2*)

Designer hotel in the former Mülheimer industrial area, close to the exhibition centre. 40 rooms, 5 lofts and 5 apartments | Deutz-Mülheimer Straße 204 | tel. 0221 4 73 30 | www.thenewyorker.de | bus 250: Danzierstraße

HOTEL SAVOY ★
(116 A3) (*ØJ G4*)

You may find a German celebrity sitting next to you at the breakfast table as this unconventionally designed hotel is popu-lar amongst actors and media people. The ● Health Club (daily 10am–11pm, bookings essential | 3 hours 18 euros) is a great place to relax. 63 rooms, 105 suites | Turiner Straße 9 | tel. 0221 162 30 | www. savoy.de | U-Bahn and buses: Breslauer Platz

ATRIUM RHEINHOTEL (0) (*ØJ 0*)

This establishment 8 km (5 mi) from the city centre is ideal if you are travelling by car. Another plus is its comfortable fur-nishings and location in a quiet side street. 48 rooms | Karlstraße 2–12 | Rodenkirchen | tel. 0211 93 57 20 | www. atriumrheinhotel.de | bus 130: Frank-straße | U 16: Rodenkirchen

BRENNER'SCHER HOF (0) (*ØJ 0*)

An 18th century estate that has been restored, its mansion is now an elegant and stylish hotel. An apartment is avail-able for long-term guests; most rooms have kitchen facilities for self-catering. The

★ **Antik-Hotel Bristol**
Spend the night in a gilt four-poster bed in this heritage building on one of the most beautiful streets in Cologne → p. 80

★ **Hotel Savoy**
This fine hotel is a popular choice among celebrity actors → p. 81

★ **Hopper Hotel et cetera**
The spartan cells of this former monastery now have luxurious interiors → p. 83

★ **Villa Hotel Rheinblick**
Beautiful view and an up-market ambience → p. 84

★ **Chelsea**
Its deconstructive architecture screams 'art'! Many artists have paid for their board and lodging with their artwork → p. 84

MARCO POLO HIGHLIGHTS

hotel is 9 km (5½ mi) from the cathedral. *41 rooms and suites | Wilhelm-von-Capitaine Straße 15–17 | tel. 0221 9 48 60 00 | www. brennerscher-hof.de | U 1: Junkersdorf*

CLASSIC HOTEL HARMONIE
(113 D1) *(ω F4)*
The deluxe rooms have air conditioning and modem connections. Relax on the roof terrace and the landscaped court-yard. If you are travelling by car, the hotel has parking spaces and garages available. *72 rooms | Ursulaplatz 13–19 | tel. 0221 165 70 | www.classic-hotel-harmonie.de | U/S-Bahn and buses: Dom/Hauptbahnhof*

ESPLANADE (112 A5) *(ω E5)*
Some interesting design elements in the foyer and breakfast room: 1950s chic with 21st century futuristic touches and feng shui elements. Elegant rooms, some with a view of the cathedral. Centrally situated and bicycles on loan for free. *32 rooms | Hohenstaufenring 56 | tel. 0221 9 21 55 70 | www.hotelesplanade.de | U-Bahn and buses: Zülpicher Platz*

LUXURY HOTELS

Excelsior Hotel Ernst
(113 D–E2) *(ω F–G4)*
An exclusive address since 1863, in the shadow of the cathedral. A large fitness room with a sauna invites you to relax. Twelve halls are available for conferenc-es, banquets, conventions and wed-dings. From 270 euros. *108 rooms and 34 suites | Domplatz | tel. 0221 27 01 | www.excelsiorhotelernst.de | U/S-Bahn and buses: Dom/Hauptbahnhof*

Le Méridien Dom Hotel ⋇
(113 E2) *(ω G4)*
Opened in 1857, this palatial building's facade is now a listed monument. Taste-ful interiors made up with a combina-tion of traditional and modern designs. 180–505 euros. *120 rooms | Domkloster 2 a | tel. 0221 2 02 40 | www.starwood hotels.com | U/S-Bahn and buses: Dom/ Hauptbahnhof*

Pullman Cologne (112 B2) *(ω E4)*
Known as the 'imperial palace' because the carnival's *Dreigestirn* (the prince, the maiden and the farmer) all stay here from the beginning of January until Ash Wednesday. From 148 euros. Also on offer is the fitness centre and sauna. Relaxed eating in the restau-rants D.Light and George M. In-house bar E.L.F. *275 rooms | Helenenstraße 14 | tel. 0221 27 50 | www.pullmanhotels. com | U-Bahn and buses: Appellhofplatz*

Hotel im Wasserturm (112 C5) *(ω F6)*
Designer hotel in a 130-year old listed building. Prices from 185–385 euros. *88 rooms | Kaygasse 2 | tel. 0221 2 00 80 | www.hotel-im-wasserturm.de | U-Bahn: Poststraße*

Hyatt Regency ⋇ (114 B4) *(ω H4)*
The bathtub in the Kennedy Suite over-looks the cathedral. The sixth floor is reserved for the exclusive Regency Club. All the rooms have modem connections, interactive TVs and Playstations. Fitness studio, sauna, steam bath and pool. 180–305 euros. *306 rooms | Kennedy-Ufer 2 a | tel. 0221 8 28 12 34 | www. cologne.regency.hyatt.com | U/S-Bahn: Deutzer Freiheit or Köln-Messe/Deutz*

FALDERHOF (0) (_ʍ 0_)

A beautiful old half-timbered house with courtyard in a secluded location, 9 km (5½ mi) from the cathedral. Lovingly furnished, cosy hotel. *33 rooms | Falderstraße 29 | tel. 02236 96 69 90 | www.falderhof. de | U 16: Sürth*

FLANDRISCHER HOF
(112 A3) (_ʍ E5_)

Only two minutes walk from Rudolfplatz. Large rooms, modern and comfortably furnished. *195 rooms | Flandrische Straße 3–11 | tel. 0221 2 03 60 | www.flandrischer hof.de | U-Bahn and buses: Rudolfplatz*

LANDHAUS GUT KEUCHHOF
(0) (_ʍ 0_)

A historically listed estate close to the Lövenich train station. From here it only takes 10 minutes by train to reach Cologne main train station. Modern furnishing in all the rooms. *43 rooms | Braugasse 14 | tel. 02234 94 60 00 | www.hotel-keuchhof. de | buses 141, 145, DB: Lövenich*

HOPPER HOTEL ET CETERA ★
(115 D5) (_ʍ D5_)

A hotel named after the artist Edward Hopper and the actor Dennis Hopper. This former monastery of the Merciful Brethren of Montabaur has designer furniture, eucalyptus parquet flooring and marble bathrooms. *49 rooms | Brüsseler Straße 26 | tel. 0221 92 44 00 | www.hopper.de | buses 136, 146: Roonstraße | U-Bahnen: Rudolfplatz*

LINT HOTEL KÖLN (113 E3) (_ʍ G5_)

This hotel is situated in the Altstadt and has a bright bistro-style space for breakfasts. Rooms are small, but modern and pleasantly furnished. *18 rooms | Lintgasse 7 | tel. 0221 92 05 50 | www.lint-hotel.de | U/S-Bahn and buses: Dom/Hauptbahnhof or Heumarkt*

HOTEL SANTO (116 B3) (_ʍ G3_)

Designer hotel close to the music college. Ten minutes walking distance from the main train station, 500 m over the bridge to the exhibition grounds. A lighting designer was used to create the hotel's special atmosphere. *69 rooms | Dagobertstraße 22–26 | tel. 0221 9 13 97 70 | www.hotelsanto.de | U-Bahn and buses: Ebertplatz*

The Dom Hotel is right next to its namesake

INSIDER TIP ▶ HOTEL VIKTORIA
(116 B2) (_ʍ G3_)

Tasteful, Victorian villa in northern Neustadt. Classic historical monument with bay-windows, marble on the walls and paintings on the ceilings and walls. *47 rooms | Worringer Straße 23 | tel. 0221 9 73 17 20 | www.hotelviktoria.com | U-Bahn and buses: Reichensperger Platz*

HOTELS: BUDGET

ACCENT HOTEL SEVERIN
(120 B1) (*∅ G7*)
Affordable well-situated hotel in the characterful Severins Quarter. Bistro restaurant. *17 rooms | Severinstraße 61 | tel. 0221 9 31 86 70 | www.hotel-accent-severin.de | U-Bahn and buses: Chlodwigplatz*

Exceptional views: art hotel Chelsea

HOTEL ARKADIA
(117 E3) (*∅ K3*)
Rustic and cosy hotel, close to the exhibition centre. *32 rooms | Gaußstraße 29–31 | tel. 0221 88 30 31 | www.hotel-arkadia.de | U 3, 4: Stegerwaldsiedlung*

CHELSEA ★
(115 D5) (*∅ E5*)
The roof area with its seven luxury rooms was designed by the architect Hartmut Gruhl in the deconstructive style. *35 rooms, 3 suites | Jülicher Straße 1 | tel. 0221 20 71 50 | www.hotel-chelsea.de | buses 136, 146: Roonstraße | U-Bahnen: Rudolfplatz*

DAS KLEINE STAPELHÄUSCHEN
(113 E–F3) (*∅ G5*)
Rustic, romantic and a historical monument. Narrow and full of nooks and crannies. Not every room has a shower and WC. *30 rooms | Fischmarkt 1–3 | tel. 0221 2 72 77 77 | www.kleines-stapelhäuschen. de | U-Bahn and buses: Heumarkt*

IM KUPFERKESSEL
(112 B1) (*∅ F4*)
This friendly, family-run hotel is simple but well-kept and close to St Gereon – a bargain for this location. *13 rooms | Probsteigasse 6 | tel. 0221 2 70 79 60 | www.im-kupferkessel.de | U-Bahn and buses: Christophstraße/Mediapark*

HOTEL REGINA
(114 B3) (*∅ B2*)
Situated in Ehrenfeld with its popular pubs and multi-cultural flair. Family-run and managed, parking in the courtyard. *17 rooms | Vogelsanger Straße 273–275 | tel. 0221 9 54 42 60 | www.regina.de | U 3, 4: Äußere Kanalstraße*

VILLA HOTEL RHEINBLICK ★ ☀
(0) (*∅ 0*)
Small villa with a plush and homely atmosphere on the Rhine. Indoor swimming pool, sauna. Breakfast is served in the beautiful conservatory. *16 rooms | Uferstraße 20 | Rodenkirchen | tel. 0221 3 40 91 40 | www.villahotel-rheinblick.com | bus 130: Uferstraße*

HOTEL WEBER (112 B5) (📖 E5–6)
Small family hotel, transport-friendly location. *27 rooms | Jahnstraße 22 | tel. 0221 27 22 99 50 | www.hotelweber.de | U-Bahn and buses: Zülpicher Platz*

FOR YOUNG PEOPLE

A&O HOSTEL KÖLN NEUMARKT
(112 B5) (📖 E5)
A former office building transformed into a hostel. Room rates (charged per person) vary according to capacity. A dorm room from 12 euros per person and single rooms from 39 euros per person. *105 private rooms, (single/double/family), 63 dorm room beds | Mauritiuswall 64–66 | tel. 0221 4 67 06 47 99 | www.aohostels. com | U-Bahn and buses: Zülpicher Platz*

YOUTH HOSTEL KÖLN-DEUTZ CITY HOSTEL (116 C5) (📖 H5)
Dorm rooms 25.30 euros for juniors, families and groups, single rooms 43 euros, double rooms 63 euros, special prices during trade fairs. *506 beds | Siegesstraße 5 | tel. 0221 81 47 11 | www.koeln-deutz. jugendherberge.de | buses 153, 170, 250, 260, U 1, 4, 9, 14: Deutz/Messe*

PATHPOINT COLOGNE (112 A5) (📖 G4)
A 1912 church that has been converted into a youth hostel. The area that was used for church services is now the common room. 5 minutes walking distance to the main station, a bed in the 8-bed room costs 17.50 euros, and in a 2-bed room 56 euros (prices for German Youth Hostel (DJH) members). *43 rooms, 165 beds | Machabäerstraße 26 | tel. 0221 13 05 68 60 | www. pathpoint-cologne.de | U 5: Breslauer Platz*

STATION HOSTEL FOR BACKPACKERS
(113 D1) (📖 F4)
Cheerful, simple rooms. From 17 euros for a 6-bed room to 39 euros in a single-bed room with bath. *50 rooms, 180 beds | Marzellenstraße 44–56 | tel. 0221 9 12 53 01 | www.hostel-cologne.de | U/S-Bahn and buses: Dom/Hauptbahnhof*

WELTEMPFÄNGER HOSTEL
(114–115 C–D3) (📖 D3)
Friendly and affordable. 600 m from the Köln-West station on the outskirts of the popular suburb of Ehrenfeld. Breakfast in the café for 4 euros, self-catering kitchen. Bring along (or rent) locks for the lockers. 6-bed room, 18 euros (weekend tariff, otherwise 17 euros), 2-bed room, 28 euros. *14 rooms | Venloer Straße 196 | tel. 0221 99 57 99 57 | www.hostel-koeln.de | U 3, 4: Piusstraße*

LOW BUDGET

▶ Five simple and welcoming rooms – all individually furnished with private washing facilities, shared shower and toilet on each floor are on offer at *Pension Otto. Richard-Wagner-Straße 18 | tel. 0221 25 29 77 | www.pensionotto.de | U-Bahn and buses: Rudolfplatz* **(115 D5)** (📖 **E5)**

▶ Also Pension Jansen *(Richard-Wagner-Straße 18 | tel. 0221 25 18 75 | www.pensionjansen.de | U-Bahn and buses: Rudolfplatz* **(115 D5)** (📖 **E5))** is situated in the Belgian Quarter with its numerous popular pubs and restaurants.

▶ Private bed and breakfast accommodation is available from *Homestay Agency Köln (Steinfeldergasse 33 | tel. 0221 130 69 00 | www.homestay-agency.de | U-Bahn: Appellhofplatz).*

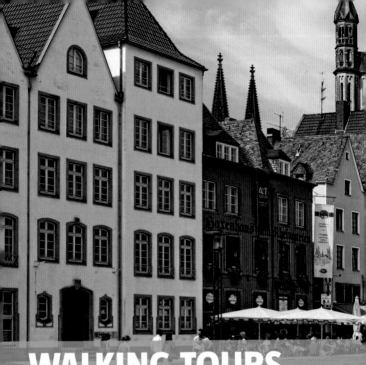

WALKING TOURS

The tours are marked in green in the street atlas, pull-out map and on the back cover

1 IN THE FOOTSTEPS OF ROMANS AND ARTISTS

The first migrants that came to Cologne where the Romans and their garrison city covered a distance of 250 acres. This route takes you along the last section of the northern side of the ancient Roman wall where some relics of the city's past are still visible. You can also experience Cologne as a city of art on this walk. The distance covered is 3 km (1.8 mi) and takes about 40 minutes.

At the north western corner of the *Domplatte*, is the **Römisches Nordtor → p. 36**, a part of the Roman city fortification, from where the main road *Cardo Maximus*, ran to the south. The architectural style of the WDR-Funkhaus broadcasting studios on Wallrafplatz is typical of the building phase in the immediate post-war period. From Wallrafplatz, turn right into An der Rechtschule Straße. At the end of the **Museum für Angewandte Kunst → p. 41** turn left into Kolpingplatz. The statue, a few feet further along, is a memorial to Adolf Kolping an ordained priest who was the founding father for the Union of Journeymen, he is also buried here. You can also see something modern here: on the corner of Drususgasse/Minoritenstraße, an abstract column by Michael Croissant

Photo: Old town with the Rheingarten and Groß St Martin

The old, the new, the sacred, the secular, the cultural and the natural: stroll through Cologne and experience a world of diversity

(1993). A few metres to the left, on the pavement in front of the church, you will see a modern sculpture by Carlo Wloch (1992). It depicts the Cologne astronomer Johann Adam Schall von Bell, who lived at the Chinese Emperor's court during the 17th century.

Cross Minoritenstraße and follow Kolumbastraße to the art museum Kolumba → p. 40. Turn right at Brückenstraße then cut across Tunisstraße and you will find yourself in Glockengasse. On the left hand side is Offenbachplatz with the opera and theatre and on the right the flagship store of 4711 – Eau de Cologne → p. 21. The route now takes you to the right, to the Neue Langasse and on the next corner to the left into Breite Straße where the DuMont-Carré → p. 68 shopping arcade awaits. The tasty treats at

Printen Schmitz → p. 66 are irresistible. The jeweller Peter Güls → p. 66 sells exclusive brands as well as his own designs.

Incidentally, St Apern Straße is the western boundary of the old Roman city. At the next corner you can still see its

The Roman tower has born witness to Cologne's history for the past 2000 years

Craving mussels? In the traditional Kölsch Bieresel → p. 56 you will find two dozen different varieties on offer during the winter. In the back area of the INSIDER TIP conservatory you will almost always find seating. For a light meal visit the pub or enjoy the lively atmosphere on the street terrace with a glass of Kölsch. A few feet further you will find the Albertusstraße with its galleries. In recent years, the art and antiques trade has become concentrated in streets like St Apern Straße. *Art Galerie 7 (St Apern Straße 7)*, show works of photographers and designers and the avant-garde is represented in the *Galerie Jöllenbeck (Nr. 40)*.

tower, the Römerturm → p. 41 with its preserved ornamental and decorative walls. Diagonally across the road you will find the *Galerienhaus* of Dr. Ralf-P. Seippel *(Zeughausstraße 26)*, which exhibits three floors of artworks by young artists from Australia and South Africa. It is now exactly 1000 m along this preserved section of the old Roman wall to get to the cathedral. The Zeughaus with its stepped gables houses the Kölnisches Stadtmuseum → p. 43, directly behind it you will find the neoclassical Römerbrunnen → p. 41. When you cross Tunisstraße, on the right hand corner you will see the remains of the Roman Lysolph Tower and this will bring you to the last stop: the Romanesque St Andreas church → p. 41, whose surroundings, the sculptor Ansgar Nierhoff designed during the 1990s.

2 VISUAL REMINDERS OF COLOGNE'S UNIQUE SPIRIT

Cologne has set up memorials, monuments and fountains for the heroes, swindlers and characters of the city. These all represent the mindset and identity of those who are indigenous to the city. This identity is also a reflection of its golden era in the Middle Ages when Cologne was Germany's largest city. You should plan to take about an hour for this next 4 km (2½ mi) walk.

The heroes of countless Kölsch jokes are honoured by the Tünnes and Schäl Monument → p. 37. Tünnes belonged to the ensemble of the Hänneschen Puppet Theatre since 1802, which was founded by Johann Christoph Winter. In 1847 his rival Franz Andreas Millowitsch also started a theatre and during this time the figure of Schäl started to appear in this puppet theatre. A few feet away, is the Schmitz Column which shows where the Romans once met the Ubii maidens and thus started the family tree of the Schmitz family – and today they take up almost eight pages in the telephone directory! When you cross the Lintgasse a passage takes you to the Ostermannbrunnen → p. 34 a fountain with figures from folksongs. Past the passage on the other side of the square you will reach Salzgasse. Turn left in the direction of the Rhine, further on, on the right hand side you will find the very narrow Tipsgasse with the Millowitsch Monument and the Hänneschen Theatre → p. 77. Although the plays are presented in Kölsch, the INSIDER TIP afternoon children's shows are really a wonderful experience.

Take the stairs down the Salzgasse to the Rhine bank. Now you can walk directly along the Rhine heading north past the Rheingarten → p. 33, underneath the bridge with a view of the old exhibition halls (today the headquarters of RTL) and the Rheinpark on the opposite side. Medieval Cologne ends at the Bastei → p. 45, the Prussian city fortification from the 19th century. However, the tower on the opposite side of the street dates back to the year 1400 and is called the Weckschnapp → p. 46. It belongs to the medieval Kunibertstorburg and was used as the city prison.

Across the Thürmchenswall and the Gereonswall you can walk along the medieval city wall, of which only the Eigelsteintorburg → p. 45 remains. From the Weidengasse → p. 47 to your left, you pass interesting junk shops and exotic Turkish shops – where you will feel as if you are in the Orient. Crossing Eigelstein and Marzellenstraße will take you back to the Dom → p. 30. At the southern end

Cologne native in bronze: Willy Millowitsch

of the *Domplatte* (Roncalliplatz) lies the Straße Am Hof with the Heinzelmännchen-Brunnen → p. 33. The tour ends at the Alten Markt, where at house no. 24, the figure of the Kallendresser → p. 28 shows his naked buttocks from his perch on the roof.

3 THE RIVER MEADOWS BY BICYCLE

The city rail Line 7 takes you from Neumarkt to the terminal at Zündorf at the south eastern edge of Cologne within 34 minutes. Bicycles are easy to take along on the train *(per person and per bicycle you will need to buy two tickets, tariff 2 b)*. A short cycle through the green meadows of the Zündorfer Groov will take about 30 min. For a longer cycle you can follow the Rhine back to Cologne inner city (15 km, approx. 9.3 mi) which will take about 60 min. Bicycles can be hired at the *Radstation am Hauptbahnhof (5 euros/3hours www.radstation koeln.de), or at Yellow Cab (10 euros/half day www.the-yellow-cab.de) or at Eco. mobility Cologne (E-Bike 24 euros/day www.eco-mobility-cologne.de).*

From the Zündorf terminal cycle right into Wahner Straße and again turn right into Schmittgasse, two streets further to the left you will find Hauptstraße. Where the road bends, you will see the 20 m (66 ft) high Zündorfer Wehrturm. A defence tower that dates back to the 12th century and is the oldest secular building in Porz. Zündorf is a district of Porz which was incorporated into Cologne in 1975. Today the tower serves as a INSIDER TIP satellite station of the Köln Stadtmuseum. Wednesdays and weekends it is open in the afternoons, when you can view exhibitions by some of Cologne's artists. *(Wed, Sat 3–6pm, Sun 2–6pm | Haupt-*

straße 181 | www.museum-zuendorfer-wehrturm.de).

Next you will need to carry your bicycle down a few steps, on the right hand side of the tower towards the Groov. The Groov is a branch of the Rhine with an island which forms a natural harbour with the main land. The word Groov comes from the Gallic word *grava* which means gravel or sandbank. Today the island is connected with the riverbank and is a recreation park.

Keep along this Rhine branch on the central street to the south up to the end of the Oberen (Upper) Groov. From here you can turn right along the peninsula and cycle through a beautiful poplar grove and then cycle back in the opposite direction to the tourist cafés and the small yacht harbour. In between this you could treat yourself to a round of mini-golf or

take a trip on one of the paddle boats. The way back to Cologne's inner city goes along the Leinpfad (towpath) alongside the Rhine to the north. At one of the many bays and beaches you can stop for a rest, a picnic or even a short sunbathe. On the other side of the river you will see the dense river woodlands of the Rhine and then the houses of Rodenkirchen.

From the Rodenkirch Autobahn Bridge you will travel a short distance through the Westhovener Aue meadows, which was once used by the Belgian armed forces as a training ground and has been left in its natural state. However, signs warn people not to leave the pathways because there may still be some old ammunition in the undergrowth.

Cycle under the bridge and past the camping site, along the Rhine in the direction of the Südbrücke, either along the embankment or directly along the Poller Wiesen, between the water and the recreation grounds.

If you prefer to take the train back from the Südbrücke, you should take the Am Schnellert road inland and in Siegburger Straße at the Poller Kirchweg station, take Line 7 in the direction Frechen. From the Südbrücke it will take 15–20 minutes to the Altstadt, while you are cycling underneath the shady trees of the Alfred-Schütte-Allee until you reach the old swing bridge on the ☀ Deutzer Werft. Here you will have a INSIDER TIP wonderful view of the Dom and the Altstadt. The massive old warehouses of the Aurora mill and the scrap yards at the Deutzer harbour will be cleared within a few years for housing similar to the Rheinau harbour development on the other side of the river.

The Groov gives the city a nautical feel: the Porz-Zündorf yacht harbour

TRAVEL WITH KIDS

ALTE FEUERWACHE (115 F3) *(ꔄ F3)*
In a converted fire station you can eat in peace on the terrace, while the children play on the climbing bars in the courtyard. *Daily from 10am | Melchiorstraße 3 | tel. 0221 73 73 93 | www.lokal-koeln.de | U-Bahn and buses: Ebertplatz | Budget*

BAUSPIELPLATZ FRIEDENSPARK (120 B2) *(ꔄ G8)*
Playground with a wooden pirate ship in the courtyard of an old fort. When the weather is bad, they can play inside in the casemate. *Mon–Fri 1–6pm | Hans-Abraham-Ochs-Weg 1 | tel. 0221 37 47 42 | www.jugz.de | U-Bahn and buses: Ubierring*

DEUTSCHER MÄRCHENWALD ALTENBURG (123 D2) *(ꔄ 0)*
The walkways of this fairytale forest have peep-boxes with scenes from Grimm's tales and Cologne's elves. *March–Oct daily 9am–7.30pm, Nov–Feb only until 4.30pm | Märchenwaldweg 15 | Odenthal-Altenberg | entrance adults 4.50 euros, children from three years 2.50 euros | tel. 02174 404 54 | www.deutscher-maerchenwald.de | from Wiener Platz bus 434 or S 11 Bergisch Gladbach, then bus 430 or by car B 51 Berliner Straße, Odenthaler Straße, Schildgen-Odenthal-Altenberg*

JOYCE MERLET PUPPENKLINIK (113 E3) *(ꔄ G5)*
For fans of old dolls, porcelain and antique toys. Buying, selling, renting and repairs. *Mon–Fri 10am–7pm, Sat until 8pm | Unter Goldschmied 3 | free entrance | www.joycemerlet.com | bus 106: Schokoladenmuseum | U/S-Bahn and buses: Dom/Hauptbahnhof*

KÖLNER KÜNSTLER THEATER (114 C3) *(ꔄ C3)*
Readings by children's authors as well as theatre pieces for 3 to 13-year olds, between 45 and 60 min. *Stammstraße 8 | tickets: 0221 5 10 76 86 | www.k-k-t.de | U 3, 4: Venloer Straße/Gürtel*

SCHOKOLADENMUSEUM (113 F5) *(ꔄ G6)*
Everything you need to know about the way in which chocolate is made from cocoa. The little ones can paint with

Where the *Heinzelmännchen* elves wait and tasty chocolate kisses lure, where pirate ships are boarded and astronauts are trained

chocolate or build small marzipan figures. The ☼ café also offers a INSIDER TIP ▶ marvellous panoramic view of Cologne *(also → p. 48).Tue–Fri 10am–6pm, Sat/Sun 11am–7pm | Rheinauhafen 1 a | entrance 7.50 euros | www.schokoladenmuseum. de | bus 106: Schokoladenmuseum, U 1, 7, 9: Heumarkt, U 3, 4: Severinstraße*

ODYSSEUM ●
(120 B2) *(ₘ K4)*

This Knowledge Adventure Park is for all age groups and has 200 activities over an area of approx. 60,000 ft². Children experience how the earth came into existence, what space looks like and how cyberspace functions. Children should be at least six years old for the astronaut training and high wire garden. *Mon–Fri 9am–6pm, Sat/Sun 10am–7pm | Corintostraße 1 | Kalk | entrance 14 euros up to 17 years, 9.50 euros up to 12 years | tel. 0221*

69 06 82 00 | www.odysseum.de | S 12, 13: Trimbornstraße, U 1, 9: Kalk-Post

VOLKSGARTEN (119 E–F2) *(ₘ E–F7)*

Here is where you can spend a summer's day with the family. This park is not far from the centre and from the beer garden you can watch the children taking rides on the paddle boats. There is also a lovely playground and lawns for picnics, playing ball and meeting new friends. *Eifelstraße/ Volksgartenstraße U 12: Eifelplatz*

WILDGEHEGE STADTWALD ●
(114 A6) *(ₘ A6)*

Peacocks, deer, geese, goats and other animals roam free in this urban woodland. During the summer there are pony rides at the eastern entrance and on weekends a small railway and train. *Daily 9am until dusk | Kitschburger Straße | U 13: Dürener Straße/Gürtel*

FESTIVALS & EVENTS

Cologne celebrates all year round. By 1400 Cologne had 110 public holidays per year. This established Cologne's reputation as light-hearted and fun-loving. The highlight of the calendar remains the carnival. The carnival starts at 11:11 on Fat Thursday (Thursday before Rose Monday) at the Alter Markt and don't even think about doing some leisurely shopping during these crazy days! Everywhere you go you will be met with party music until Tuesday, when at precisely midnight a straw doll *(Nubbel)* is burned outside the pubs.

PUBLIC HOLIDAYS

1 Jan, *Good Friday, Easter Monday,* **1 May,** *Ascension Day, Whit Monday, Corpus Christi;* **3 Oct** *(German Unity Day);* **1 Nov** *(All Saints);* **25 and 26 Dec**

EVENTS

JANUARY

▶ INSIDERTIP ▶ *Peoples' session of the* **KG Alt Köllen** in a tent in Neumarkt mid Jan. Very colourful. *www.alt-koellen.de* The ▶ INSIDERTIP ▶ *Stunksitzung* is the 'alternative' carnival. It has a cabaret-style feel with lots of sarcasm and satire. *www.stunksitzung.de*

FEBRUARY

▶ ● *Street carnival:* the largest parades are the ▶ *Schull- un Veedelszöch* on carnival Sunday and the Rose Monday parade

MARCH

▶ *Lit.Cologne:* international literary festival with events in the Literaturhaus in the Mediapark, in bookshops, theatres and pubs. *www.litcologne.de*

APRIL

▶ ★ *Art Cologne:* 180 galleries exhibit art in the Koelnmesse. *Tel. 0221 82 10 | www.artcologne.com*

MAY

▶ *Hänneschen-Kirmes:* face-painting and carnival bands on the Eisenmarkt. *www.haenneschen.de*

JUNE

▶ *Mülheimer Gottestracht:* during Corpus Christi floats travel from Mülheim along

Cologne's event calendar is filled with art and spectacle – and not just during the carnival

the Rhine in the direction of the Dom
▶ INSIDER TIP *Edelweißpiratenfestival:* a massive music festival in Friedenpark with reggae, folk and *Kölschrock*. www.edel weisspiratenfestival.de

JULY

▶ ★ ● *Sommer Köln:* open air concerts, theatre, films, children's programmes. Venues and times: www.sommerkoeln.de
▶ *Christopher Street Day:* crazy and colourful parade for lesbians and gays
▶ *Kölner Lichter:* big firework display with music along 6 km (4 mi) of the Rhine banks. Upcoming dates: 14 July 2012, 13 July 2013, 19 July 2014. *www.koelner-lichter.de*

AUGUST

▶ *c/o pop:* festival of electronic music that takes place over five days in various Cologne clubs. www.c-o-pop.de

SEPTEMBER

Alternating exhibits: digital /projection technology at ▶ *Photokina*, or years with unequal digits ▶ *bicycle and motorbike exhibition IFMA* (tel. 0221 82 10).

OCTOBER

▶ *Racecourse Weidenpescher Park:* the highlight of the racing season is the *Preis des Winterfavoriten*. www.koeln-galopp.de
▶ *International Köln Comedy Festival:* 120 fun-filled events. www.koeln-comedy.de

NOVEMBER

▶ *Elfter im Elften:* opening of the carnival session at Heumarkt/Alter Markt

DECEMBER

▶ *Christmas markets* at Neumarkt, Roncalliplatz, Alter Markt and Rudolfplatz
▶ *New Year:* the best view of the fireworks is from the Deutzer Bridge

LINKS, BLOGS, APPS & MORE

LINKS

▶ www.cologne-tourism.com The official tourism site with comprehensive listings for exhibitions, events, insider tips, package deals on selected events and even a tourist hotline!

▶ www.rhinemagazine.com Is an online English language magazine bringing readers the best of the Rhine. Aimed at locals as well as tourists, it includes listings for cultural events, news, general interest articles as well as information on local services and cultural mores

BLOGS & FORUMS

▶ english-speaking-cologne.blogspot.com Is a site set up for the English speaking community of Cologne and is also a useful resource for tourists, with pictures, an online chat forum and a map listing all the 'English friendly stuff' in Cologne

▶ www.english-network.de This is the Bonn English Network website that offers information and a social network for English speakers in the areas around Bonn and Cologne. Information on events, clubs and associations, ideas on what to do and where to go as well as social gatherings

▶ americanincologne.wordpress.com Is a blog by an American from Florida who has moved to Cologne with her German husband. The blog is about her new life and includes a link to her photo blog: expatinpictures.wordpress.com

VIDEOS

▶ www.audiotravel.com/cologne-city-guide For an mp3 Audio tour of the city with some insider information about all the major tourist sites

Regardless of whether you are still preparing your trip or already in Cologne: these addresses will provide you with more information, videos and networks to make your holiday even more enjoyable

STREAMS

▶ www.tripfilms.com/Travel_Video-v206-Cologne-Cologne_Cathedral-Video.html For a three-minute video about the architecture and history of Cologne's world famous cathedral

▶ www.koeln-altstadt.de/koeln-service/webcamsinkoeln/index.html Selection of nine webcams that are distributed over the city's major tourist attractions

APPS

▶ Cologne Travel Guide Tripwolf is an up-to-date mobile travel guide travel app which offers access to expert advice from Marco Polo and others publishers. It also has ratings and reviews from other travellers from the Tripwolf community

▶ Cologne Walking Tours and Map This app is ideal to use to explore the city at your own pace and aims to make you feel as though you are being taken around by a local guide. Covers all the city's famous landmarks, sites, monuments and museums

NETWORK

▶ www.travelpod.com/s/cologne?st=user For some first-hand reports, travel blogs, photos and a wide selection of videos by other international Cologne tourists

▶ twitter.com/VisitKoeln For up-to-the-minute tweets about what is happening in Cologne

▶ www.couchsurfing.org Do some online surfing and click your way onto a couch in Cologne. A great way to connect with locals and experience the city in a more personal way. Not only is the bed (or sofa) free but you also get to meet new people

TRAVEL TIPS

ARRIVAL

✈ The Konrad Adenauer Airport Köln-Bonn is 15 km (approx. 9 mi) from Cologne city centre. A taxi ride to the cathedral should take about 20 min (price approx. 30 euros) and from the main train station the S 13 and RE 8 take about 20 minutes to the Köln/Bonn airport station. Price: approx. 2.40 euros. From Düsseldorf airport it takes about 45 to 60 min to Cologne. Taxi: approx. 75 euros, S-Bahn approx. 10 euros, IC 18.50 euros.

🚗 Expect traffic jams during rush hour, major events and fairs. Incentive parking (park-and-ride) is clearly indicated. During carnival days, alcohol checks are the order of the day in and around the city centre and many suburban detour roads are closed. In the inner city area between the Rhine and inner Kanalstraße only vehicles with special environment stickers are allowed.

RESPONSIBLE TRAVEL

It doesn't take a lot to be environmentally friendly whilst travelling. Don't just think about your carbon footprint whilst flying to and from your holiday destination but also about how you can protect nature and culture abroad. As a tourist it is especially important to respect nature, look out for local products, cycle instead of driving, save water and much more. If you would like to find out more about eco-tourism please visit: *www.ecotourism.org*

🚆 Important to remember: some ICE trains only stop at Köln-Hauptbahnhof, and some only go from the Ruhr district via Köln-Deutz to Frankfurt am Main. There are taxi stands at both exits of the Hauptbahnhof. The U/S-Bahn station Dom/Hauptbahnhof is situated on the cathedral side. You can reach the Altstadt or Eigelstein Quarter in just a few minutes by foot.

BICYCLE RENT

KÖLNER FAHRRADVERLEIHSERVICE
(113 F4) (*ω G5*)
To hire a bicycle costs 2 euros per hour, 10 euros per day. A three hour guided city roundtrip takes place daily (15 euros, including bicycle). English language guides available with prior arrangement. *Markmannsgasse/Rheingarten, directly at the Deutzer Brücke | tel. 0171 6 29 87 96 | www.koelnerfahrradverleih.de | U-Bahn and buses: Heumarkt*

BOAT TRIPS

Explore Cologne by water with a river boat trip and get some wonderful views of the riverbanks and the old city. ● The *Müllemer Böötche* sails from the Hohenzollernbrücke to Rodenkirchen. If you have some spare time, you can also leave the city and go on a relaxing day tour to the Siebengebirge.

BONNER PERSONEN-SCHIFFAHRT
(116 B3) (*ω G–H3*)
From the Bastei (*Mon, Tue, Wed, mid July–mid Sept, during the main holiday season July–mid Aug also Sat/Sun*) is a passenger boat trip to Linz and back. *Departure 9.30am, return 6.45pm | approx. 24 euros | tel. 0228 63 63 63 | www.b-p-s.de*

From arrival to weather

Holiday from start to finish: the most important addresses and information for your Cologne trip

DAMPFSCHIFFAHRT COLONIA
(113 F2) (*ⓜ G4*)

The famous *Müllemer Böötche*: enjoy the one hour journey from the Hohenzollern-brücke-Zoo-Mülheim and back. *April–Oct 10am–5.30pm. Every 45 min during week-ends, longer time delays during the week* | 7.30 euros | tel. 2 57 42 25 | www. dampfschiffahrt-colonia.de

FÄHRBETRIEB HANS LINDEN
(113 F2) (*ⓜ G4*)

Ferry from Hohenzollernbrücke to the exhibition centre/Rheinpark. *April–Oct 10am until approx. 5.30pm (depending on weather) and exhibition schedules* | return ticket 3 euros | tel. 38 47 38

KÖLN-DÜSSELDORFER DEUTSCHE RHEINSCHIFFAHRT AG (113 F3) (*ⓜ G5*)

From Frankenwerft/Rheingarten (between Hohenzollern-/Deutzer Brücke) a one hour trip is available on two ships; the *MS Jan von Werth* and the *MS Drachenfels*. *Daily 7.80 euros, midnight trip (2 hrs) daily 11.10 euros, evening trip Wed/Thu 13 euros, Sat with buffet 46.80 euros; daily trip to Zons 19.20 euros* | specific times under www. koeln-duesseldorfer.com | tel. 2 08 83 18

KÖLNTOURIST PERSONENSCHIFFAHRT
(113 F2) (*ⓜ G4*)

Leaves from Konrad-Adenauer-Ufer: one hour trip to Rodenkirchen. *March-Oct from 10.15am, Nov/Dec from noon, last trip during summer 5.40pm* | 7.30 euros | www. koelntourist.net

CARNIVAL

Trying to get something done in Cologne during carnival is not easy: all the city's

BUDGETING

Kölsch	1.50–1.60 euros for a glass (0,2 l)
Parking	1.80–3 euros for an hour in a car park
U-Bahn	1.70 euros for three stops
Carnival	30–45 euros entrance to the carnival session
Coffee	2.10–2.55 euros for a cup
Halve Hahn	4.10–4.50 euros for a portion

public authorities and official bodies are closed or use skeleton staff. If you want to join in with the festivities at the street or pub carnivals then it is best to leave your credit card and valuable jewellery in the hotel safe and do not take any 100 euro-notes. Tickets for the balls and meetings are available from 2 January from the *Kaatebus* or ticket bus on the Neumarkt. Dress warm for the four-hour long parade on Rose Monday. Some 1.5 million spectators line the 6 km (3.6 mi) long parade route: so be there on time to have a good view.

CONSULATES

BRITISH CONSULATE
Yorckstraße 19 | 40476 Düsseldorf | tel. 02 11 94480

CANADIAN CONSULATE
Benrather Straße 8 | 40213 Düsseldorf | tel. 02 11 172170

US CONSULATE GENERAL

Willi-Becker-Allee 10 | 40227 Düsseldorf | tel. 0211 7888927

CUSTOMS

EU citizens may import and export goods for their own personal use tax-free. Duty-free for non-EU citizens are: 50g perfume, 2 l wine, 1 l spirits and 200 cigarettes.

EMERGENCY CALLS

Police: tel. 110 | Fire brigade: tel. 112

EMERGENCY SERVICES

Night pharmacy: *Apotheken-Notdienst | tel. 118 80*
Medical emergencies: *tel. 118 80*
Dental emergencies: *Medeco Zahnklinik Köln (daily 7am–10pm | Ludwigstraße 1 | tel. 0221 27 26 50)*

IMMIGRATION

No visa is necessary for EU citizens to travel to or to work in Germany. Non-EU citizens require a visa (valid up to 90 days) or a residence permit.

INFORMATION

KÖLN TOURISMUS (113 D2) *(ⅉ F4)*
Directly opposite the cathedral is the tourist service centre and souvenir shop. Telephonic hotel bookings *Mon–Sat 8am–8pm, Sun and public holidays 10am–5pm | tel. 0221 22 13 04 00 | commission per booking 3 euros for personal bookings in the service centre. Telephonic bookings free.* Business hours at the Tourist Info at the cathedral: *Mon–Sat 9am–8pm, Sun and public holidays 10am–5pm | tel. 0221 22 13 04 00- | info@koelntourismus.de | www.koeln.de.*

A calendar with the most important dates with sections like concerts, films, theatre, literature, art and parties, can be found at: *www.koelner.de*; Weather: *www.wetterbote.de/koeln*; official site of the city council: *www.stadt-koeln.de;* ticket reservations: *www.koeln-ticket.de*; exhibitions: *www.koeln-galerien.de*, *www.museenkoeln.de*; fairs: *www.koeln-messe.de*; carnival: *www.koelnerkarneval.de*

PARKING

The car park at the cathedral costs 0.60 euro per 20 min, max. 18 euros per day *(evening rate from 7pm 1 euro/hour.)*. Other places in the inner city charge 1.50–1.80 euros per hour and the Agrippabad car park charges 3 euros/hour. Tip: instead of using the parking Dom/Rhein, use the parking **INSIDER TIP** directly at Heumarkt or Gürzenich. Watch out for the temporary parking restrictions that are put up on the eve of the carnival and street festivals: the tow-away truck appears faster than you think! And getting involved in a discussion with a meter maid in Cologne is futile. Blocking a bicycle path or a fire engine parking place is also a towable offence. In the car parks you should also not leave anything valuable lying around in your car for thieves to see.

PHONE & MOBILE PHONE

The international dialling code for Germany is 0049, the area code for Cologne is (0) 221. Dial 0044 for Great Britain followed by the area code without '0' and 001 for USA and Canada. There are four main providers in Germany: T-Mobile (D1), Vodafone (D2), E-Plus (coverage of the E-Net is not as good as D-Net) and O2. Germany operates on a GSM network.

PUBLIC TRANSPORT

Due to permanent traffic jams on the Cologne Autobahn ring and endless parking problems, it is best to to use public transport in the Cologne-Bonn-Düsseldorf region. Tickets in the regional transport system are valid to Düsseldorf, Mönchengladbach or Wuppertal (tariff zone 5).

You are charged according to your destination, e.g. Königswinter or Zons and the rate is the same no matter whether you use the DB-Regionalexpress, the S-Bahn, the tram and buses of the Kölner Verkehrs-Betriebe (KVB) or the Stadtwerke Bonn (SWB) or the Regionalverkehr Köln GmbH (the DB travels twice as fast as the KVB to Bonn): from Cologne main station a trip to Bonn takes 23 min and to Düsseldorf 30 min. Tickets can be bought at the ticket counter at the main train station, in the passenger centre (e.g. at Neumarkt), at the vending machines at the tram and the stations. A *Kurzticket* for three stops costs 1.70 euros, a normal ticket 2.50 euros, and a 4 man ticket 9 euros.

With a City-Ticket (2.50 euros) you can travel for 90 minutes and change over as often as you like. Get a Regio-Ticket to Düsseldorf price range 5 (9.90 euros). A day ticket, although more expensive (21.40 euros), is worthwhile because you can travel the whole day until 3am. *Info: www.kvb-koeln.de*

REGIONALVERKEHR KÖLN GMBH
(113 D–E1) (*W G4*)
From the Hauptbahnhof/Breslauer Platz buses travel to the outskirts of Cologne. *Tel. 163 70 | www.rvk.de*

SIGHTSEEING TOURS

AE-EVENT (114 B5) (*W B5*)
Specific guided tours (brewery with beer tasting, night tours, Romanesque churches, etc.) with pre-arrangement in different foreign languages (from 8 people). Bookings and prices: *www.ae-event.de/*

CURRENCY CONVERTER

£	€	€	£
1	1.20	1	0.85
3	3.60	3	2.55
5	6	5	4.25
13	15.60	13	11
40	48	40	34
75	90	75	63.50
120	144	120	102
250	300	250	212.5
500	600	500	425

$	€	€	$
1	0.80	1	1.25
3	2.40	3	3.75
5	4	5	6.25
13	10.40	13	16.25
40	32	40	50
75	60	75	93.75
120	90	120	150
250	200	250	312.50
500	400	500	625

For current exchange rates see www.xe.com

calendar. *AE-event Agentur für Erlebnisevent und Tourismus UG | Aachener Straße 352 | tel. 16 82 98 09 or 0175 2 57 71 43 | kontakt@ae-event.de*

CCS BUSREISEN GMBH
(113 D2) (*W F4*)
City tours. *Daily 10am, noon, 2pm, April–Oct also Fri/Sat 4pm | 11 euros, from Köln Tourismus | Kardinal-Höffner-Platz 1 | tel. 9 79 25 70 71 | www.ccs-busreisen. de | U/S-Bahn and buses: Dom/Hauptbahnhof*

DOMFORUM

(113 D2) *(ⓜ F4)*

Guided tours through the cathedral and the famous twelve Romanesque churches. The bi-annual programme with monthly dates and times can be obtained free of charge in the Domforum or from *www. domforum.de. Domkloster 3 | tel. 92 58 47 30 | U/S-Bahn and buses: Dom/ Hauptbahnhof*

FLIGHT TRAINING COLOGNE

(0) *(ⓜ 0)*

For everyone who likes historical planes, book a nostalgic trip around Cologne, Bonn or the Bergischen Land area in an original Antonov *(booking calendar www. ft-cgn.de). 30 min cost 80–158 euros. From March to end Oct departure from Hangelar (Siegburg), from Cologne/Bonn only with at least nine guests. Tel. info and bookings: 0151 16 75 10 76*

LIFEFLIGHT

A 30 min round flight from Bonn-Hangelar over Cologne from 156.25 euros. After an advance payment/transfer you can print your ticket as a PDF document. Flights mostly take place on Saturdays, at least four people per booking. *Marienburger Straße 44 | tel. 07 00 54 33 35 44 | www. lifeflight.de*

STATTREISEN – CITY TOURS

Something a little different from the usual tourist programmes. Themed tours are offered like *Cologne in Tales and Legends* and other excursions through the city quarters. *Duration approx. 9 euros/2hrs | times and venues: www.stattreisen-koeln.de | office: Bürgerstraße 4 | info-tel. 73 80 95*

TOUR-AGENTUR

Themed adventure tours through the city like the pilgrimage tour, the cemetery

WEATHER IN COLOGNE

	Jan	Feb	March	April	May	June	July	Aug	Sept	Oct	Nov	Dec
Daytime temperatures in °C/°F	4/39	6/43	10/50	14/57	19/66	22/72	24/75	24/75	20/68	14/57	9/48	5/41
Nighttime temperatures in °C/°F	–1/30	0/32	2/36	5/41	8/46	12/54	14/57	14/57	11/52	7/45	4/39	0/32
Sunshine hours/day	2	2	4	5	6	7	6	5	5	4	2	2
Precipitation days/month	18	15	13	17	13	13	14	14	14	16	18	17

tour, the literature tour or the criminal tour offers some entertainment and mystery. Group tours cost between 109 and 145 euros. *Tour-Agentur | Hohe Pforte 22 | tel. 9 32 72 63 | info@tour-agentur.de | www.colonge-guided-tours.com*

SWIMMING POOLS & ICE SKATING

AQUALAND
(0) (𝓜 0)

Swimming pool with water slide and a certain Caribbean flair, sauna, solarium and fitness centre. *Mon–Thu 9.30am–11pm, Fri 9.30am–midnight, Sat 9am–midnight, Sun 9am–11pm, Mon/Wed from 7pm nudists | 2 hrs 9.90 euros, day ticket 14.90 euros | Merianstraße 1 | Chorweiler | tel. 7 02 80 | www.aqualand.de | U 18: Chorweiler Zentrum*

CLAUDIUS-THERME
(116–117 C–D3) (𝓜 J3)

Thermal baths in the Rheinpark, indoor and outdoor pools, physical therapy (hot mud etc.). *Daily 9am–midnight | 2 hrs 14.50 euros, weekends and public holidays 16.50 euros, day ticket 27.50/29.50 euros | Sachsenbergstraße 1 | Deutz | tel. 98 14 40 | www.claudius-therme.de | U/S-Bahnen: Deutzer Bahnhof, then bus 150*

EIS- UND SCHWIMMSTADION/ LENTPARK
(116 B2) (𝓜 G2)

Re-opened in autumn 2011 after renovations with indoor and outdoor swimming pools, sauna and ice rink. *Lentstraße 30 | contact: KölnBäder GmbH | tel. 178 24 62 | www.koelnbaeder.de | U 5, 18: Reichenspergerplatz*

MÜNGERSDORFER STADION
(0) (𝓜 0)

Cologne's biggest pool with eight swimming pools and a 10 m (32 ft) tower. *Mid May–Sept Mon–Fri 10am–8pm, Sat/Sun 9am–8pm, during school holidays from 10am | Aachener Straße/Stadion | tel. 2 79 18 40 | www.koelnbaeder.de | U 1: Stadion*

TAXI

Starting price 2.65 euros, 6am–10pm, up to 5 km (3 mi) every km 1.65, every further km 1.40 euro, 10pm–6am up to 5 km (3 mi) every km 1.75 euro, every further km 1.50 euro; waiting time per minute 0.40 euro, credit card payment (surcharge) 1.00 euro. The night tariff is the same for Sundays and public holidays (as at print deadline). When calling from a hotel or restaurant, bank on a 5–10 minute waiting time. Heavy duty taxis for extensive luggage should be booked in advance. Christmas Eve from 7pm, New Year's Eve and during carnival days, taxis are hard to find after midnight. *Tel. Taxi-Ruf Köln 28 82* or download the free mytaxi app from *www.mytaxi.net* and book your taxi with your smartphone.

TICKETS

KÖLN MUSIK TICKET SHOP
(113 E2) (𝓜 G4)

Mon–Fri 10am–7pm, Sat 10am–4pm | tel. 20 40 81 60 | Roncalliplatz (at the Roman-Germanic Museum) | U/S-Bahn and buses: Dom/Hauptbahnhof. Another pre-sale ticket office: *www.koelnticket.de.*

TIPPING

If you are satisfied with the service you should tip between 10 and 15 per cent. Many taxi drivers are in the habit of adding their tip. The Köbesse (waiters) in the pubs are not allowed to drink on the job so it's best not to buy them a round. Municipal employees, museum and city guides are not allowed to accept tips.

USEFUL PHRASES GERMAN

PRONUNCIATION

We have provided a simple pronunciation aid for the German words (see the square brackets). Note the following:

ch	usually like ch in Scottish "loch", shown here as [kh]
g	hard as in "get"
ß	is a double s
ä	like the vowel in "fair" or "bear"
ö	a little like er as in "her"
ü	is spoken as ee with rounded lips, like the French "tu"
ie	is ee as in "fee", but ei is like "height", shown here as [ei]
'	stress on the following syllable

IN BRIEF

Yes/No/Maybe	Ja [yah]/Nein [nein]/Vielleicht [fee'leikht]
Please/Thank you	Bitte ['bi-te]/Danke ['dan-ke]
Sorry	Entschuldige [ent'shul-di-ge]
Excuse me, please	Entschuldigen Sie [ent'shul-di-gen zee]
May I ...?/ Pardon?	Darf ich ...? [darf ikh]/Wie bitte? [vee 'bi-te]
I would like to .../ have you got ...?	Ich möchte ... [ikh 'merkh-te]/ Haben Sie ...? ['hab-en zee]
How much is ...?	Wie viel kostet ...? [vee-feel 'koss-tet]
I (don't) like this	Das gefällt mir/nicht [das ge-'felt meer/nikht]
good/bad	gut/schlecht [goot/shlekht]
broken/doesn't work	kaputt [ka-'put]/funktioniert nicht/ funk-tsion-'eert nikht]
too much/much/little	(zu) viel/wenig [tsoo feel/'vay-nikh]
Help!/Attention!/ Caution!	Hilfe! ['hil-fe]/Achtung! [akh-'tung]/ Vorsicht! ['for-sikht]
ambulance	Krankenwagen ['kran-ken-vaa-gen]/ Notarzt ['note-aatst]
police/fire brigade	Polizei [pol-i-'tsei]/Feuerwehr ['foy-er-vayr]
danger/dangerous	Gefahr [ge-'far]/gefährlich [ge-'fair-likh]

GREETINGS, FAREWELL

Good morning!/afternoon!/evening!/night!	Gute(n) Morgen ['goo-ten 'mor-gen]/Tag [taag]/ Abend ['aa-bent]/Nacht [nakht]
Hello!/Goodbye!	Hallo ['ha-llo]/Auf Wiedersehen [owf 'vee-der-zayn]

Sprechen Sie Deutsch?

"Do you speak German?" This guide will help you to say the basic words and phrases in German.

See you!	Tschüss [chüss]
My name is ...	Ich heiße ... [ikh 'hei-sse]
What's your name?	Wie heißt Du [vee heist doo]/ heißen Sie? ['heiss-en zee]
I'm from ...	Ich komme aus ... [ikh 'ko-mme ows]

DATE & TIME

Monday/Tuesday	Montag ['moan-tag]/Dienstag ['deens-tag]
Wednesday/Thursday	Mittwoch ['mit-vokh]/Donnerstag ['don-ers-tag]
Friday/Saturday	Freitag ['frei-tag]/Samstag ['zams-tag]
Sunday/holiday	Sonntag ['zon-tag]/Feiertag ['fire-tag]
today/tomorrow/ yesterday	heute ['hoy-te]/morgen ['mor-gen]/ gestern ['gess-tern]
hour/minute	Stunde ['shtun-de]/Minute [min-'oo-te]
day/night/week	Tag [tag]/Nacht [nakht]/Woche ['vo-khe]
What time is it?	Wie viel Uhr ist es? ['vee-feel oor ist es]
It's three o'clock	Es ist drei Uhr [ez ist drei oor]

TRAVEL

open/closed	offen ['off-en]/geschlossen [ge-'shloss-en]
entrance (vehicles)	Zufahrt ['tsoo-faat]
entrance/exit	Eingang ['ein-gang]/Ausgang ['ows-gang]
arrival/arrival (flight)	Ankunft ['an-kunft]/Abflug ['ap-floog]
toilets/restrooms / ladies/gentlemen	Toiletten [twa-'let-en]/ Damen ['daa-men]/Herren ['her-en]
(no) drinking water	(kein) Trinkwasser [(kein) 'trink-vass-er]
Where is ...?/Where are ...?	Wo ist ...? [vo ist]/Wo sind ...? [vo zint]
left/right	links [links]/rechts [rekhts]
straight ahead/back	geradeaus [ge-raa-de-'ows]/zurück [tsoo-'rük]
close/far	nah [naa]/weit [veit]
taxi/cab	Taxi ['tak-si]
bus stop/ cab stand	Bushaltestelle [bus-hal-te-'shtell-e]/ Taxistand ['tak-si- shtant]
parking lot/parking garage	Parkplatz ['park-plats]/Parkhaus ['park-hows]
street map/map	Stadtplan ['shtat-plan]/Landkarte ['lant-kaa-te]
airport/ train station	Flughafen ['floog-ha-fen]/ Bahnhof ['baan-hoaf]
schedule/ticket	Fahrplan ['faa-plan]/Fahrschein ['faa-shein]
I would like to rent ...	Ich möchte ... mieten [ikh 'mer-khte ... 'mee-ten]
a car/a bicycle	ein Auto [ein 'ow-to]/ein Fahrrad [ein 'faa-raat]
a motorhome/RV	ein Wohnmobil [ein 'vone-mo-beel]
a boat	ein Boot [ein 'boat]

petrol/gas station	Tankstelle ['tank-shtell-e]
petrol/gas / diesel	Benzin [ben-'tseen]/Diesel ['dee-zel]
breakdown/repair shop	Panne ['pan-e]/Werkstatt ['verk-shtat]

FOOD & DRINK

Could you please book a table for tonight for four?	Reservieren Sie uns bitte für heute Abend einen Tisch für vier Personen [rez-er-'vee-ren zee uns 'bi-te für 'hoy-te 'aa-bent 'ein-en tish für feer pair-'zo-nen]
The menu, please	Die Speisekarte, bitte [dee 'shpei-ze-kaa-te 'bi-te]
Could I please have ...?	Könnte ich ... haben? ['kern-te ikh ... 'haa-ben]
with/without ice/	mit [mit]/ohne Eis ['oh-ne eis]/
sparkling	Kohlensäure ['koh-len-zoy-re]
vegetarian/allergy	Vegetarier(in) [veg-e-'taa-ree-er]/Allergie [al-air-'gee]
May I have the bill, lease?	Ich möchte zahlen, bitte [ikh 'merkh-te 'tsaa-len 'bi-te]

SHOPPING

Where can I find...?	Wo finde ich ...? [vo 'fin-de ikh]
I'd like .../I'm looking for ...	Ich möchte ... [ikh 'merkh-te]/Ich suche ... [ikh 'zoo-khe]
pharmacy/chemist	Apotheke [a-po-'tay-ke]/Drogerie [dro-ge-'ree]
shopping centre	Einkaufszentrum [ein-kowfs-'tsen-trum]
expensive/cheap/price	teuer ['toy-er]/billig ['bil-ig]/Preis [preis]
more/less	mehr [mayr]/weniger ['vay-ni-ger]
organically grown	aus biologischem Anbau [ows bee-o-'lo-gish-em 'an-bow]

WHERE TO STAY

I have booked a room	Ich habe ein Zimmer reserviert [ikh 'haa-be ein 'tsi-me rez-erv-'eert]
Do you have any ... left?	Haben Sie noch ein ... ['haa-ben zee nokh]
single room	Einzelzimmer ['ein-tsel-tsi-mer]
double room	Doppelzimmer ['dop-el-tsi-mer]
breakfast/half board	Frühstück ['frü-shtük]/Halbpension ['halp-pen-si-ohn]
full board	Vollpension ['foll-pen-si-ohn]
shower/sit-down bath	Dusche ['doo-she]/Bad [baat]
balcony/terrace	Balkon [bal-'kohn]/Terrasse [te-'rass-e]
key/room card	Schlüssel ['shlü-sel]/Zimmerkarte ['tsi-mer-kaa-te]
luggage/suitcase	Gepäck [ge-'pek]/Koffer ['koff-er]/Tasche ['ta-she]

BANKS, MONEY & CREDIT CARDS

bank/ATM	Bank/Geldautomat [bank/'gelt-ow-to-maat]
pin code	Geheimzahl [ge-'heim-tsaal]
I'd like to change ... euros	Ich möchte ... Euro wechseln [ikh 'merkh-te ... 'oy-ro 'vek-seln]

cash/credit card	bar [bar]/Kreditkarte [kre-'dit-kaa-te]
bill/coin	Banknote ['bank-noh-te]/Münze ['mün-tse]

HEALTH

doctor/dentist/ paediatrician	Arzt [aatst]/Zahnarzt ['tsaan-aatst]/ Kinderarzt ['kin-der-aatst]
hospital/ emergency clinic	Krankenhaus ['kran-ken-hows]/ Notfallpraxis ['note-fal-prak-sis]
fever/pain	Fieber ['fee-ber]/Schmerzen ['shmer-tsen]
diarrhoea/nausea	Durchfall ['doorkh-fal]/Übelkeit ['ü-bel-keit]
inflamed/injured	entzündet [ent-'tsün-det]/verletzt [fer-'letst]
prescription	Rezept [re-'tsept]
pain reliever/tablet	Schmerzmittel ['shmerts-mit-el]/Tablette [ta-'blet-e]

POST, TELECOMMUNICATIONS & MEDIA

stamp/letter	Briefmarke ['brief-maa-ke]/Brief [brief]
postcard	Postkarte ['posst-kaa-te]
I'm looking for a prepaid card for my mobile	Ich suche eine Prepaid-Karte für mein Handy [ikh 'zoo-khe 'ei-ne 'pre-paid-kaa-te für mein 'hen-dee]
Do I need a special area code?	Brauche ich eine spezielle Vorwahl? ['brow-khe ikh 'ei-ne shpets-ee-'ell-e 'fore-vaal]
Where can I find internet access?	Wo finde ich einen Internetzugang? [vo 'fin-de ikh 'ei-nen 'in-ter-net-tsoo-gang]
socket/adapter/ charger/wi-fi	Steckdose ['shtek-doh-ze]/Adapter [a-'dap-te]/ Ladegerät ['laa-de-ge-rayt]/WLAN ['vay-laan]

LEISURE, SPORTS & BEACH

bike/scooter rental	Fahrrad-['faa-raat]/Mofa-Verleih ['mo-fa fer-lei]
rental shop	Vermietladen [fer-'meet-laa-den]
lesson	Übungsstunde ['ü-bungs-shtun-de]

NUMBERS

0 null [null]	10 zehn [tsayn]	20 zwanzig ['tsvantsikh]
1 eins [eins]	11 elf [elf]	50 Fünfzig ['fünf-tsikh]
2 zwei [tsvei]	12 zwölf [tsvölf]	100 (ein) Hundert ['hun-dert]
3 drei [drei]	13 dreizehn [' dreitsayn]	200 Zwei Hundert [tsvei 'hun-dert]
4 vier [feer]	14 vierzehn ['feertsayn]	1000 (ein) Tausend ['tow-zent]
5 fünf [fünf]	15 fünfzehn ['fünftsayn]	2000 Zwei Tausend [tsvei 'tow-zent]
6 sechs [zex]	16 sechzehn ['zekhtsayn]	10 000 Zehn Tausend [tsayn 'tow-zent]
7 sieben ['zeeben]	17 siebzehn ['zeebtsayn]	
8 acht [akht]	18 achtzehn ['akhtsayn]	½ ein halb [ein halp]
9 neun [noyn]	19 neunzehn ['noyntsayn]	¼ ein viertel [ein 'feer-tel]

NOTES

MARCO POLO TRAVEL GUIDES

- PACKED WITH INSIDER TIPS
- BEST WALKS AND TOURS
- FULL-COLOUR PULL-OUT MAP
  AND STREET ATLAS

STREET ATLAS

The green line ▬ indicates the Walking tours (p. 86–91)

All tours are also marked on the pull-out map

Photo: Alfred-Schütte-Allee on the Rhine riverbank

Exploring Cologne

The map on the back cover shows how the area has been sub-divided

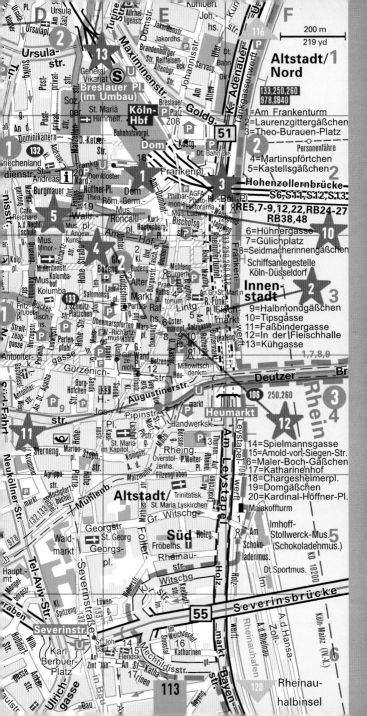

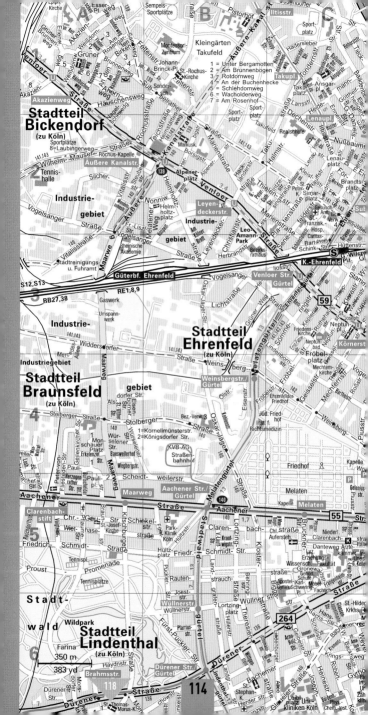

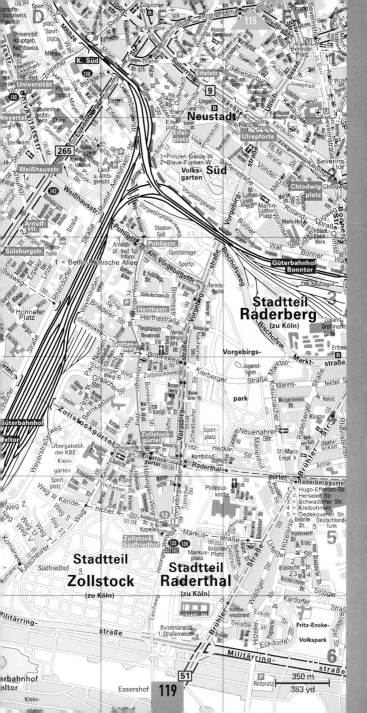

This is a map page (page 119) showing the Köln districts of **Neustadt Süd**, **Stadtteil Raderberg (zu Köln)**, **Stadtteil Zollstock (zu Köln)**, and **Stadtteil Raderthal (zu Köln)**.

Selected labels visible on the map:

- Universität
- Studentenwohnheim
- Weißhausstr.
- Arnulfstr.
- Sülzburgstr.
- Tennishalle
- Honnefer Platz
- Güterbahnhof Eifeltor
- K. Süd
- Eifelstr.
- 9 Neustadt
- Volksgarten
  - 1 = Prinzen-Garde-W.
  - 2 = Blaue-Funken-W.
- Süd
- Ulrepforte
- Chlodwigplatz
- Severinstor
- Stadion-Süd
- Pohligstr.
- Sportanlage
- 1 = Berlin-Rheinische Allee
- Herthastr.
- Theophanostr.
- Gottesweg
- Güterbahnhof Bonntor
- Stadtteil Raderberg (zu Köln)
- Zollamt
- Großmarkthalle
- Eritrea
- Vorgebirgsstraße
- Jugendheim
- Kierberger Straße
- park
- Zollstockgürtel
- Übergabebf. der KBE
- Kleingärten
- Sportplatz
- Rosenzweigweg
- Sportplatz
- Fritz-Hecker-Str.
- Kombibad
- Raderthal
- Neuenahrer Str.
- St.-Maria Empf. K
- Raderberggürtel
  - 1 = Hugo-Efferoth-Str.
  - 2 = Herseler Str.
  - 3 = Schwadorfer Str.
  - 4 = Kreibohrmstr.
  - 5 = Oedekovener Str.
- Deutschlandfunk
- Stadtteil Zollstock (zu Köln)
- Zollstock Südfriedhof
- Südfriedhof
- Kapelle
- Markusplatz
- Philippuskirche
- Stadtteil Raderthal (zu Köln)
- Heeresamt
- Bundesanstalt f. Straßenwesen
- Kreiswehrersatzamt
- Fritz-Encke-Volkspark
- Kardorfer Str.
- Militärring
- Reitplatz
- 350 m
- 383 yd
- Essershof
- 51

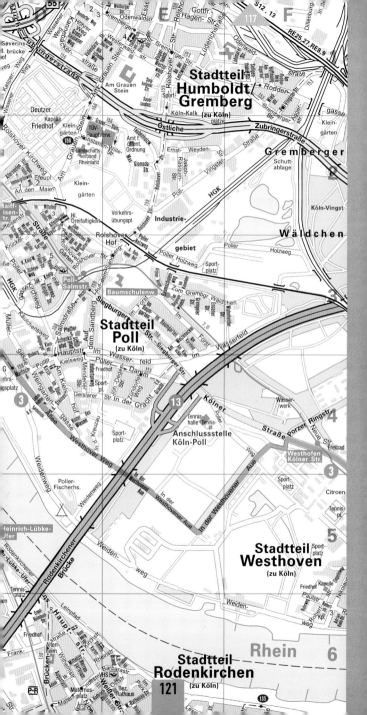

E

S12·13

F

117

RE25·27·RE8·9

Stadtteil Humboldt/Gremberg (zu Köln)

Deutzer

Kapelle Friedhof

Klein-gärten

Kölner-Kalk

Östliche

Zubringerstraße

Klein-gärten

Gremberger

TÜV-Hauptverw.

Landschafts-verband Rheinland

Amt f. öffentl. Ordnung

Ernst-Weyden-Str.

Jakob-Rasquin-Str.

Schutt-ablage

Köln-Vingst

Klein-gärten

Hl. Dreifaltigkeit

Verkehrs-übungspl.

Industrie-

gebiet

Poller Holzweg

Sport-platz

Holzweg

Wäldchen

Rolshover Hof

Poll-Salmstr.

Baumschulenw.

Zum Grembg. Wäldchen

Stadtteil Poll (zu Köln)

Siegburger Str.

Im Baumschen

Wasser-feld

Wasserfeld

Poller Friedhof

Köln-Poll

Kölner

Tennis-halle

Tennis-pl.

Anschlussstelle Köln-Poll

Wasser-werk

Straße Porzer Ringstr.

3

Sport-platz

13

Freibad

3

Westhofen Kölner Str.

Citroen

Tennis-pl.

Sport-platz

Stadtteil Westhoven (zu Köln)

Sport-platz

Friedh. Kapelle

Paulstr.

Poller-Fischerhs.

Weiden-weg

In der Westhovener Aue

Heinrich-Lübke-Ufer

Rodenkirchener Brücke

Weiden-weg

Weiden-

Tennis-platz

Leinpfad

Friedhof

Frank-

Rhein

5

6

Stadtteil Rodenkirchen (zu Köln)

P+R

Bez. Rathaus

121

135

This index lists a selection of the streets and squares shown in the street atlas

KEY TO STREET ATLAS

Motorway with number
Autobahn mit Nummer
Autoroute avec numéro

Motorway junction number
Nummer der Autobahnanschlussstelle
Numéro d'echangeur d'autoroute

Expressway/ Federal road
Schnellstraße/ Bundesstraße
Route express/ Route nationale

Main through road
Durchgangsstraße
Grande route

Other roads/ Footpath
Übrige Straßen/ Weg
Autres routes/ Sentier

Roads under construction/ projected
Straßen in Bau/ Planung
Routes en construction/ en projet

Pedestrian zone/ One-way street
Fußgängerzone/ Einbahnstraße
Zone piétonnière/ Rue à sens unique

Town and communal boundary
Stadt- und Gemeindegrenze
Limite de ville et commune

Environmental zone
Umweltzone
Zone environnement

Railway with station
Eisenbahn mit Bahnhof
Voie ferrée avec gare

Freight and industrial railway
Güter- und Industriebahn
Voie ferrée de marchandise et industrielle

Rapid transit train with number and station
S-Bahn mit Nummer und Station
Train en trafic suburbain avec numéro et gare

Underground/ Light Rail
U-Bahn/ Stadtbahn
Métro/ Métro Léger

Bus/ Tramway with terminus
Bus/ Straßenbahn mit Endhaltestelle
Autobus/ Tramway avec terminus

Car park/ Parking house/ Under-
ground car park
Parkplatz/ Parkhaus/ Tiefgarage
Parking/ Garage/ Parking souterrain

Park+Ride/ Parking control system
Park+Ride/ Parkleitsystem
Park+Ride/ Système de signalisation

Walking tours
Stadtspaziergänge
Promenades en ville

Indoor swimming pool
Hallenbad
Piscine couverte

Church
Kirche
Église

Hospital
Krankenhaus
Hôpital

Camping site/ Youth hostel
Campingplatz/ Jugendherberge
Camping/ Auberge de jeunesse

Post office
Post
Bureau de poste

Forester's lodge
Försterei
Maison forestière

Isolated trees
Einzelne Bäume
Arbres isolés

Inn/ Excursion-Inn
Wirtshaus/ Ausflugslokal
Auberge/ Café-Restaurant

Transmitting station/ Lighthouse
Sendeanlage/ Leuchtturm
Station d'émission/ Phare

Monument/ Tower
Denkmal/ Turm
Monument/ Tour

Windmill/ Windpower
Windmühle/ Windrad
Moulin à vent/ Éolienne

Tourist information center
Tourist-Information
Syndicat d'initiative

Consulate/ Embassy
Konsulat/ Botschaft
Consulat/ Ambassade

Forest/ Park, Cemetery
Wald/ Park, Friedhof
Forêt/ Parc, Cimetière

Vineyard
Weinberg
Vignoble

Heath/ Marsh, Swamp
Heide/ Moor, Sumpf
Lande/ Marais, Marécage

MARCO POLO Highlights

INDEX

This index lists all places and sights, plus the names of important people featured in this guide. Numbers in bold indicate a main entry.

WRITE TO US

e-mail: info@marcopologuides.co.uk

Did you have a great holiday?
Is there something on your mind?
Whatever it is, let us know!
Whether you want to praise, alert us
to errors or give us a personal tip –
MARCO POLO would be pleased to
hear from you.
We do everything we can to provide the
very latest information for your trip.

Nevertheless, despite all of our authors'
thorough research, errors can creep in.
MARCO POLO does not accept any
liability for this. Please contact us by
e-mail or post.

MARCO POLO Travel Publishing Ltd
Pinewood, Chineham Business Park
Crockford Lane, Chineham
Basingstoke, Hampshire RG24 8AL
United Kingdom

PICTURE CREDITS
Cover photograph: Cathedral and *Domplatte*, Look: Lubenow
DuMont Bildarchiv: Fischer (51, 92/93); © fotolia.com: David Gallun (16 centre); R. Freyer (22, 35, 74, 84);
GOODLACK Fassadenkunst a la ART: Ron Voigt (16 bottom); R. Hackenberg (front flap left, front flap right, 2 top,
2 centre top, 2 centre bottom, 4, 6, 7, 9, 10/11, 15, 18/19, 26/27, 33, 34, 45, 67, 69, 76, 89, 96 top, 97, 129);
S. Kallnbach (1 bottom); L. Kornblum (2 bottom, 3 top, 3 centre, 3 bottom, 8, 12, 24 left, 24 right, 25, 38, 40, 48,
52, 54/55, 56, 59, 60 left, 62/63, 64, 70/71, 72, 78/79, 88, 90/91, 96 bottom, 106/107); Laif: Gollhardt&Wieland
(92, 93), Huber (36, 42/43, 83, 94), Linke (5, 20, 30, 47, 80, 94/95, 95); le bloc: Martin Förster (17 top); Look:
Lubenow (1 top); MadameMiamMiam: Sandra Schlesinger (16 top); mauritius images/imagebroker: Creativ Studio
Heinemann (60 right), Falkenstein (86/87); Ucon-lodge: Stefan Huben, info@studio2000.eu (17 bottom)

1st Edition 2012
Worldwide Distribution: Marco Polo Travel Publishing Ltd, Pinewood, Chineham Business Park,
Crockford Lane, Basingstoke, Hampshire RG24 8AL, United Kingdom. Email: sales@marcopolouk.com
© MAIRDUMONT GmbH & Co. KG, Ostfildern
Chief editor: Marion Zorn
Author: Jürgen Raap; editor: Jens Bey
Programme supervision: Ann-Katrin Kutzner, Nikolai Michaelis, Silwen Randebrock
Picture editor: Gabriele Forst, Stefan Scholtz
What's hot: wunder media, München
Cartography street atlas and pull-out map: © MAIRDUMONT, Ostfildern
Design: milchhof : atelier, Berlin; Front cover, pull-out map cover, page 1: factor product munich
Translated from German by Wendy Barrow; editor of the English edition: Margaret Howie, fullproof.co.za
Prepress: M. Feuerstein, Wigel
Phrase book in cooperation with Ernst Klett Sprachen GmbH, Stuttgart, Editorial by Pons Wörterbücher

DOS & DON'TS ✋

A few things to bear in mind in friendly Cologne

DO CALL THE WAITER KÖBES

It doesn't matter if the waiter in the blue jacket's name is Albert or Peter: you simply call them 'Köbes' (pronounced: cur-bes).

DON'T ORDER TEA IN A BRAUHAUS

Your answer to that will be: *'Mer sin en Brauhaus un kein Sanatorium!'* (We are in a pub, not a sanatorium!). The Köbes will react just as rudely if you order a glass of mulled wine. But the worst: ordering *Altbier* a beer from Düsseldorf – that will mean the end of the *Kölsch* humour.

DO PAY STRAIGHT AWAY

While it is not the usual way of doing things, on Rose Monday you will have to pay for your Kölsch (or any drink) as soon as it arrives.

DO BE WARY OF DETOURS

Some taxi drivers feel that it is their duty to show tourists half of the Rhineland. So you should never let the taxi driver know that it is your first time in Cologne.

DON'T DODGE FARES

Never forget to stamp your ticket! Ticket inspectors are inconspicuous in their everyday clothes and extremely diligent and merciless when they catch a fare-dodger on the tram or anywhere else.

DO PARK LEGALLY

The meter maids are on the lookout for parking offenders until 11pm (even in the suburbs). If you park illegally on the bicycle track, fire engine zone or in a handicapped space, your car will be towed away and you will be slapped with a hefty 100 euro fine.

DON'T GIVE THIEVES OPPORTUNITIES

As in every large city, you should stay aware and be careful. Extra care should be taken at the main station, around the cathedral and at Christmas markets and major events. Pickpockets, swindlers and thieves have a field day in these areas.

DO AVOID THE RHINE BANKS AT NIGHT

The Rhine bank promenade north of the Hohenzollern Bridge is not the safest place for an evening stroll.

DO TAKE IT WITH A PINCH OF SALT

A friendly local may say, 'Do visit me sometime!' and although it may sound like a genuine invitation, do not get too excited. Such an invitation from a Rhinelander is not always meant seriously.